SMITH

Riding to win

DATE DUE			

Riding to Win

EPH SMITH

Riding to Win

STANLEY PAUL *London*

STANLEY PAUL & CO LTD
178–202 Great Portland Street, London W1

AN IMPRINT OF THE HUTCHINSON GROUP

London Melbourne Sydney
Auckland Bombay Toronto
Johannesburg New York

★

First published 1968

This book has been set in Times, printed in Great Britain on Antique Wove paper by Anchor Press, and bound by Wm. Brendon, both of Tiptree, Essex

09 085760 7

To
DOREEN

ACKNOWLEDGMENT

I should like to express my thanks to Michael Borissow of Southern News Services Ltd., Maidstone, Kent, for his assistance in the compilation of this book.

Contents

Illustrations

I

Success with Blue Peter

I MUST have been mad. Stark, staring mad. It was the morning of the Derby of 1939, I had the greatest chance ever of winning on Blue Peter, and there I was in the paddock at my father's farm, riding a hunter 'over the sticks'.

One fall, one slip and I could have been tossed, trodden on, kicked or suffered a broken neck. Why I did it I do not know. I can only say it was a mark of my confidence at that time, and, thankfully, I did not fall or get a kick. After an hour's jumping with two or three horses I went in for breakfast as though it was any ordinary day of the week.

But, of course, Derby Day is no ordinary day. For one thing, it is a national institution. Nearly every man, woman and child old enough to read takes an interest in it. More bets are struck, more interest is shown, more words are spoken and written about it and more people go to this sporting event of the year than to any other in the country, including the Grand National and the Cup Final.

Usually there are up to a quarter of a million people on Epsom Downs for the race. They arrive from dawn. Some have been there from the previous night to get a good position on the rails. Hundreds of open-top buses and special coaches line the course and two funfairs start up hours before the first race along with the fortune-telling gypsies, tipsters, men wrestling in chains, stallholders, beer-tent merchants, jellied-eel and ice-cream vendors and tented-public-lavatory attendants. Pearly Queens start dancing before midday and hours before the race bookmakers are shouting the odds on the runners in the greatest horse race in the world.

On special trains to Tattenham Corner, Epsom Downs and Epsom itself, thousands of Derby Day supporters flock to the course with coach-loads of travellers from all over the country and thousands more motorists who jam the roads from early light to get to the meeting.

It's a holiday for everyone, from the East End families with their cheerful kids to the top-hatted gentry and their fashionably turned-out ladies who may drink champagne and eat smoked salmon in the private boxes of the huge grandstand, which towers above the horseshoe-shaped course like some ant-infested monster.

There is no day like it anywhere in the world. The excitement, the air of expectancy and optimism, the shouts, the calls and the noise all combine to create an atmosphere of tension unlike anything else I have experienced.

Yet that day in 1939 was, for me, one of the calmest of my life. Oh yes, there were a few butterflies in my stomach, but I had never felt more confident about anything than that Blue Peter would win.

It was a beautiful day in every respect. A blazing sun drenched the whole of the Downs and only a slight heat haze marred what was otherwise perfect visibility. All the bookies and spectators on the popular stands and across the Downs were in shirt-sleeves and with the ladies in their sleeveless dresses this added even more colour to the already brilliant scene.

In the dressing room I pulled on Lord Rosebery's

primrose-and-pink silks and cap, the same ones worn by jockey Danny Maher to win the 1905 Derby on Cicero for Lord Rosebery's father, and sat down quietly on a bench until it was time to go out.

After driving to the course in my car I had ridden inconspicuously in the first two races and, although I had had to change silks, I still had thirty-five minutes to wait before the start by the time I had passed the clerk of the scales.

After I had weighed out, Roger Paris, the head lad of Mr. (now Sir) Jack Jarvis's stable, came across, took my saddle and went away with it to the parade ring.

It was a beautifully polished, well-worn saddle and I thought: Well, I hope it brings me the same kind of luck as its former owner had in this race.

For it had been owned until fairly recently by the great jockey Freddie Fox, who had twice won the Derby while riding with it, on Cameronian in 1931 and Barham in 1935. When he retired he sold the saddle to my brother Doug and, needing a stone saddle for the Derby to ride at nine stones, I had borrowed it from him. (He has ridden hundreds of winners on it since.)

After Roger had gone I sat down, smoked a cigarette and chatted quietly to one or two of the other jockeys.

It is a strange atmosphere in the dressing room before the Derby. Everyone seems keyed up and there is an air of great tension. Some of the jockeys cannot sit still and keep jumping up, walking round nervously and then sitting down again. Others look agitated and worried, looking in the mirror and fiddling with their silk mufflers to make sure they are right or nervously checking that their silks are tucked in properly and there is no mark on their already shining black riding boots.

I just sat there. Looking back, it seemed incredible how

calm I was and how unconcerned I must have looked.

Fred Rickaby, brother of Bill and now a successful trainer in Durban, South Africa, came across and sat next to me.

'Well, Eph, who's going to win?' he asked.

Without a moment's hesitation I replied: 'I will, Fred. I'll win it.'

He blinked a little at my extreme confidence, but he only nodded quietly. He knew that Blue Peter was not only 7—2 favourite but was also reputed to be a super horse.

The minutes ticked by slowly and I still sat quietly, smoking a second cigarette and waiting . . . just waiting for the moment when we should all stand up and move out. My brother Doug came across. 'Good luck. Have a nice ride,' he said.

'Thanks. You too,' I answered.

At last the bell went and everyone stood up and started to move out of the dressing room, across the weighing room and through the double glass doors into the winning enclosure to walk out to a line of taxis waiting alongside the rails. At Epsom the parade ring is nearly 250 yards from the dressing room and these taxis are always laid on to take the jockeys down to the horses.

The tempo outside was beginning to warm up now, bookies were shouting the odds more fervently, everyone seemed to be talking at once and the noise from the people on the Downs seemed like the buzz from a hundred bee-hives. With the sound of bells and music from the hurdy-gurdies and a few cheers as we jockeys appeared the whole atmosphere was vibrant and electric.

The taxi ride took no more than a couple of minutes and I quickly spotted Jack Jarvis talking to Lord Rosebery in the centre of the parade ring as the runners were being walked around them by the lads from each stable represented.

I shook hands with Lord Rosebery and my trainer. They looked far less confident than I was, and both were perspiring freely.

There were thirty-two runners and Mr. Jarvis said: 'You are drawn No. 26, Eph. It's a good draw towards the outside and there isn't much I need to tell you. Just stay handy and when you get into the straight, come on.'

I nodded, glanced towards Blue Peter and was comforted to see that he looked absolutely perfect. He was walking round quite calmly, was not sweating at all, and with his long, lazy stride and rippling muscles seemed as fit as it was possible for a horse to be.

The bell rang again and I went slowly across to the horse, to be helped on by Roger. I checked the stirrups, adjusted them, took a look round and started to move about the parade ring before being let out on to the course for the final parade in front of the stands.

At Epsom, for the mile-and-a-half races, the horses have to be led up the course towards the winning post. They go past this for about a furlong before the lads let them go, and then canter back down towards the parade ring and the stables to turn left on to the path which leads into a dip and up, across the Downs, to the start which is opposite the stands.

This parade is always a trying moment for horses and riders on Derby Day. The noise of the crowd, the music, the atmosphere and the tension seems to affect many of them. The horses are inclined to get excitable, might break out into a sweat and the jockeys have to be 100 per cent alert to keep them calm and under control.

But for me, that day, the Gods were smiling. Blue Peter walked up the course as though it were an every-day occurrence. While some of the other horses were dancing and prancing he looked as happy and as comfortable as the policeman's hack walking along in front.

It was the same all the way to the start. He moved easily into a canter to reach the path, and then trod his way as delicately as a ballet dancer down the slope and up the other side to reach the starting gate on the far side of the Downs.

One by one the horses arrived to gather in a rough circle and walked around while the starter's assistant darted in and out, checking girths and tightening them up. The starter, Captain Allison, called the roll, we answered our names with monosyllabic 'Yes, sirs', and then he moved over towards his rostrum.

The jockeys started to form into a rough line and the white flag went up.

Over the loudspeaker system the words 'They're under starter's orders' echoed across the Downs from the grandstand and, as though a 50,000-volt shock had cut through everyone, 250,000 voices hushed into an uncanny silence.

I found my place between horses drawn Nos. 25 and 27 and still Blue Peter was as calm as though he was on Newmarket Heath waiting for a gentle gallop. He moved forward into line and it was a first time go. No sooner had we got within a couple of yards of the tapes than they shot up and all thirty-two of us were away in a very good line.

Blue Peter jumped off well as soon as I kicked him out and I headed towards the right-hand side rail to go the shortest way. The first half-mile is an uphill run, swinging gently to the right, and then, as the course starts to level out, it turns gently to the left. After the mile post it starts to turn more sharply to the left, going downhill until you reach

(*The Field*)

Eph Smith relaxing in the garden of his home at Newmarket shortly after his retirement

(Sport & General)

Eph with his son Robin, when a young child, at the December sales

(John Slater)

'My wonderful dog, Dan'

Tattenham Corner four furlongs from home and finally swings sharply left into the straight.

Immediately after the start I found myself in about eighth position on the right-hand rail and I tucked Blue Peter in until we had covered about 600 yards and it was time to move into the centre of the course before easing over to the left-hand rail at the mile post.

I could feel Blue Peter striding along coolly and easily and I was still as confident as ever. After a mile I took up about fifth position, a little on the outside and slightly behind two of the other four leading horses to make sure that I did not get shut in at any time. We were going a fair gallop, but I did not mind being away from the rails as I was not worried about my horse's stamina.

Passing the short piece of course on the right which leads to the seven-furlong start we began to go downhill and the pace quickened. Blue Peter followed the leaders quite freely and, in fact, gained a place as one of them dropped back a bit. At the top of the hill going down into Tattenham Corner I was still fourth but, if anything, Blue Peter was going more smoothly than ever.

Many horses do not like racing down the hill, start to get their legs crossed and lose their stride or falter. Blue Peter had raced on the course before to win the Blue Riband Trial and I felt sure he would act on the course again. Sure enough, he went down the hill just as if he were an engine on rails, keeping a perfectly balanced stride, and by the time we reached Tattenham Corner he was lying third, only about two lengths behind the leading horse, Heliopolis, ridden by my old friend Dick Perryman.

Dick was going well and his horse was striding out strongly, but I knew by now that I was sure to win, barring accidents. As I gripped the reins I could feel that

Blue Peter still had so much in hand it was quite incredible. He felt as if he had enough strength to go on for ever.

Almost immediately after turning into the straight there is a path across the course for pedestrians to cross on to the Downs and which is covered with peat. In recent years some jockeys have complained that these crossings are liable to upset a horse and make it lose its stride. But Blue Peter could not have cared less about the peat or the crossing. With perfect timing he took it in his stride and started to close the gap on Heliopolis.

With just under two furlongs to go I felt now was the time to clinch it. I changed my hands, gathered the reins in more tightly, and Blue Peter took hold of the bit without the slightest hesitation to lengthen his stride instantly. He swept past the second horse and then Perryman's mount in less than twenty yards, as if they were both standing still.

The winning post seemed to be coming to meet me instead of me going towards it and when I kicked my horse gently on with hands and heels he swept on like an express train. He never showed any signs of weakening, he was never challenged, I never had to touch him with the whip and he won by four lengths.

Second was Fox Cub II (100—6) ridden by Gordon Richards and Heliopolis was third at 100—8. After ten years as a jockey I had won the Derby and reached the pinnacle of success!

It was a wonderful feeling. I don't think I was as excited as when I rode my first winner, but I was delighted that our confidence in the horse had been realised. Lord Rosebery came to lead me in and his first words were: 'Well done, Smith.' He was still sweating and when I saw Jack Jarvis beaming and perspiring too I thought they had had a much worse race of it than me. In the dressing room there were handshakes and shouts of congratulation and I ordered champagne for everyone. All sorts of spivs and people I didn't know seemed to get in for this free booze-up and I received a bill for £50 afterwards. Not that I could have cared.

I had to get ready for the next race and one of the most touching things said during the whole day came that afternoon from Brownie Carslake, who was senior jockey at that time. We rode down to the parade ring together and he said quietly: 'Well done, son. You have done something I have never done—won the Derby.'

Lord Rosebery arranged for me to receive ten per cent of the winnings through Wetherby's, and also, in a very thoughtful gesture, had one of Blue Peter's racing plates mounted on an onyx base and he presented it to me.

I had given a full description of the race to racing correspondents soon afterwards and then the B.B.C. asked me to speak on the radio that evening. But I had always shied away from publicity and turned the offer down.

After all the excitement had died away I didn't really know what to do. My girl friend Doreen Moore (whom I married the following February and with whom I have lived so happily ever since, God bless her) was at the meeting and was staying with the Fred Winter family at Epsom.

Jack Jarvis had always told me that if he ever won the Derby he would give a party at the Piccadilly Hotel and, true to his word, arranged one for that night and asked me to attend.

There were other offers to go to this and that function from all sorts of people, but none of them were much to my liking.

It seemed to me that I ought to be back in Berkshire in my home country, the area where I had been brought up, where I knew so many genuine people and where I had first learned to ride and hunt.

I told Doreen how I felt, and she wisely understood and stayed on at Epsom. Mr. Jarvis said he was sorry I could not attend his gathering but appreciated my sentiments too.

As quietly as I could I slipped away to my car in the jockeys' park on the Downs and drove off almost unrecognised by the home-going crowds.

It was just as I wanted it.

That night I cracked a bottle of champagne at home with my family and then went on a pub crawl with my father and Doug. It was just the kind of celebration I liked, drinking beer and chatting with old pals, and one of the first people I had a drink with was my former school headmaster, Mr. Bradfield, at the Bee Hive at White Waltham.

I got a bit tight, drinking nothing but beer, but was in bed by half past ten. It had been a fantastic day and quite suddenly it hit me that I was very, very tired.

Almost as soon as my head touched the pillow I was asleep.

2

Early Years

THE 4th of May was my mother's birthday and everyone had been hoping that little Eph would also arrive on that date in 1915. But Mum and Dad had just about given up all hope of having two birthdays in one family on the same day when I arrived in good order just before midnight.

Yes, it was a photo-finish at the start for me and life has been like that ever since on race courses all over the country; exciting, full of kicks, full of 'near things' and with plenty more photo-finishes thrown in for good measure.

Now, after thirty-seven years in the saddle, I have taken doctor's good advice and decided to retire. I shall still be riding work to keep fit with some of the Newmarket trainers who have become my friends over the years, but the glamour and glitter of the racing days on courses from Ascot to Ayr and Brighton to Beverley are over for me.

Racing has been very good to me and there are only a few of the really big races I have not won. In those thirty-seven years I rode a total of 2,313 winners, including the Derby, the 2,000 Guineas and the Eclipse Stakes on Blue Peter—the finest horse I ever rode—and the St. Leger on Premonition.

Only four other jockeys in the history of British racing have ever ridden more winners: Sir Gordon Richards (4,870), my brother Doug Smith (3,102) (Sept. 1967), the great Fred Archer (2,748) and George Fordham (2,587).

My number of winners could probably have been greater, but I was happy to be retained by only two people—trainer Mr. Jack Jarvis and, since 1949, by Mr. H. J. Joel. They were both extremely good to me and although I could probably have had more than 18,000 rides in those years if I had 'shopped around' for other first retainers, there seemed no need to do so. I was happy with them and they, apparently, were satisfied with me.

Not that I haven't ridden for many other owners and trainers over the years. The Queen, the late King George VI, Lord Milford, Lord Willoughby de Broke, Sir Winston Churchill, Lord Derby, Lord Rosebery and many others have put me up.

They haven't always been horses with much chance, and I've often made myself unpopular by saying so, but at least it was a pleasure to be asked to ride them for such distinguished owners and lovers of the turf.

I have only two regrets: that my health gave way in the winter of 1965 which caused me to retire a couple of years earlier than I might have wanted to and that I never won the Oaks officially. I say 'officially' because I always feel that when my horse West Side Story crossed the line alongside the French challenger Monade the verdict should have been a 'dead-heat'. The record books show that Monade was given the verdict. What they don't say is that it took the judge fourteen minutes to reach a decision, that he consulted four or five photographs before doing so and that, even then, it was barely possible to split the horses.

If the judge could split them to his satisfaction, then I suppose the verdict was right. But in my view if any decision is as close as that then the verdict should be a 'dead-heat'.

However, you can't win them all in any game and I

can always dine out on the story of that race and finish up with the tongue-in-the-cheek, self-satisfying last line: 'I wuz robbed.'

Although I was not exactly born in the saddle, it wasn't very long before I was in one, as a diminutive three-year-old. My father, Ernest Smith, was a sporting farmer and undoubtedly spent more time thinking and worrying about horses than he did on farming our 200 acres at Pondwood Farm, Shottesbrooke, near Maidenhead. He was madly keen on hunting and worried the life out of my mother with the number of injuries he suffered through falls. He was a thickset, jovial man, nearly six feet tall, and I was still unable to walk properly when he gave me my first introduction to the equestrian arts.

One day, when the Garth Hunt, so famous for its following in the Berkshire countryside, cut across our farm, my dad made a slight deviation into our yard, picked up young Eph and continued on his way in pursuit of the fox. My mother was horrified to see me perched excitedly in front of him on his saddle, but by the time she had gathered breath to protest he had jumped his horse in one massive leap over a ditch, a hedge *and* a plough, which he had not seen standing on the far side of the hedge until airborne. That horse must have been a great jumper!

My father was quite fearless on the horse and won over fifty races in point-to-point meetings all over Berkshire, Wiltshire, Hampshire and Buckinghamshire. Not until later in life (he died in 1960) did he suffer any serious ill-effects when the number of fractured bones he had incurred started to stiffen up and he was crippled.

We were not a wealthy family by any means, but life at Pondwood was always full of fun, the discipline was never harsh or too strict and my childhood was such that

I can look back on it without any clouds of unhappiness spoiling the scene.

There was always something going on, whether connected with horses, shooting, or hunting, and some of the meals cooked by my mother still linger deliciously on the palate. For instance, we had sparrow-and-blackbird pie on many occasions, a delightful dish if properly cooked and prepared, and my mother was an expert. Our job was to catch the sparrows, which we did mostly in a barn near our farmhouse, at night, with the aid of a torch. The birds used to settle for the night in the barn and when we crept in with the torch and shone it on them they remained transfixed long enough for us to catch them with our bare hands.

It was not from Dad that I got my physique as a jockey —I'm just four feet eleven inches tall—so it must have been inherited from my mother, who was always slight and rather frail. No, Dad just started me off on the road to love horses and after that first hectic two-hour ride with the hunt he encouraged me in every way to keep on riding.

Later, in fact, he regularly incurred the wrath of the school attendance officer by turning a blind eye when I played truant from White Waltham County Council School so that I could take part in gymkhanas and horse shows all over the county.

Mother used to say that if the attendance officer had as many erring pupils as my elder brother Charlie, Doug and myself then they ought to take the school round to the pupils, rather than the pupils going to the school.

As well as hunting horses, Dad used to deal in them and frequently went to Reading market for this purpose. One day he came home with a really beautiful pony for Charlie, who was five years older than I. She was called Gladys, was only thirteen hands, but turned out to be a wonderful jumper and a great little animal for hunting.

In fact she became famous for her ability in the hunting field and at shows all over the South of England.

Then, to everyone's surprise, Dad arrived home from the market one day with a donkey. He had paid £2 for it. 'It's company for the pony,' he told everyone, proudly. But that donkey turned out to be the most incredible 'company'. In no time at all it was almost outshining the pony as a hunter, as a jumper and even as a polo mount.

We called it Sansovino after the Derby winner, and I doubt if anyone, before or since, has had a donkey like it. For a start it could race like a two-year-old, better than some, if you like, because it never played about at the start. One kick and it would tear off at full speed without the slightest hesitation.

It could jump its own height, or more, and we built a special fence and a water jump for it in the paddock. The fence eventually became a transportable fence, for the fame of the jumping-racing-hunting donkey spread so much we were flooded with requests to give demonstrations of the animal's capabilities at different types of shows all over the place.

When we first entered her in a Donkey Derby—they were held frequently in those days—she won so easily that I think all the other owners must have thought she'd been doped! But next time out she won just as easily and there just wasn't another donkey anywhere that could stand up to her.

At one meeting there was supposed to be a Donkey Derby over a mile—twice round the track—for the best donkeys in the South. Sansovino set off at a gallop, was a hundred yards in front after doing the first quarter of a mile and finally crossed the finishing line on her second circuit when the other donkeys were crossing the line at the end of their first circuit.

After that Sansovino was banned from all Derbies. The organisers said: 'You must not enter her. If you do, no one else will compete.'

So Sansovino had to be content with her demonstrations and her hunting.

I think I was about five when I first went out hunting with her and it was an amazing experience. She kept going all day. No obstacles could stop her and if she couldn't get over a hedge she just got down on her knees and barged her way through. I'd jump off her back, crawl through a hole in the hedge and she'd follow like some bulldozing ferret. Her objective was to stay as close to the hounds as possible and she won a string of admirers with the Garth Hunt and the Berks and Bucks Staghounds.

But she also had some opposition from a rather toffee-nosed set which used to come down from London to join the hunt. They thought the idea of a donkey out hunting with them was 'just not the thing, don't you know', particularly when it was ridden by a little boy who could keep up as well as them.

One of the leading followers of the Garth Hunt was the racehorse trainer Miss Norah Wilmot, of Binfield. She was a great fan of the donkey's and a champion of mine too. Miss Wilmot has always had an expressive vocabulary and I remember on one occasion she tore a tremendous strip off one of the London women who was annoyed about the donkey starting to go through a gate at the same time as she was trying to get through it on her expensive and well-groomed hunter.

'Get that frightful animal out of the way,' she said to me.

Miss Wilmot heard every word. And in two short, sharp sentences she told the lady what she thought of her, what she ought to know about good manners and where she could put her la-di-da ways.

No one ever protested about the donkey within Miss Wilmot's hearing again!

I even used Sansovino as a polo pony on occasions, bandaging his legs in proper fashion and riding on our own makeshift polo pitch at Pondwood, and she always put up a good performance, even against the ponies ridden by my father and elder brother Charlie. In fact, I used to spend hours with her, grooming her and rubbing her down.

I rode in my first gymkhana before I went to school, on a pony called Pickles. Quite often it was necessary to ride ten or fifteen miles to get to the shows, but I always enjoyed riding rather than going to school. At my first show, in the contest for the best boy rider, the girths around my pony broke while in mid-air over the little fence.

Somehow I managed to stay on and they gave me first prize. I think there was a bit of ill-feeling about the award at that show, at Mortimer, near Newbury, because I don't suppose I was the best rider at all. Still, they gave me the prize and that was all that mattered to young Eph.

It was nothing to us lads to get home at ten or eleven at night from these shows, so it's hardly surprising that the school attendance officer was paying frequent calls on my folks.

However, we did go to school sometimes and our conveyance was a trap pulled by another donkey, which belonged to my cousins. They lived at a neighbouring farm and this was a remarkable donkey too. It pulled the trap without any reins and had terrific road sense. It used to set off at a gallop and sometimes it would continue to gallop all the way, much to our delight. While we were in school it would rest in a nearby blacksmith's yard and then it would gallop us all back home again.

Unlike Sansovino, this donkey hated having anyone ride her. She didn't mind pulling the trap, but passengers on her back were definitely unwelcome. She would buck, leap, and turn almost inside out to dislodge any would-be rider and my father won many a fiver bet with people who thought they could stop on her—but couldn't!

Sansovino did not much like being in a trap and when harnessed in would try to set off at the same gallop as in the Donkey Derbies. The trap would rattle, sway from side to side and finally she went so fast that she usually overturned it. On one occasion I was thrown clear on to the grass verge, and looked up to see her still tearing towards our farmyard with great gusto, the shafts of the trap still attached.

The same thing happened when my father made us a sleigh out of an old rocking horse. Doug, who was then about six, took it in turns with me to ride. On one occasion the donkey galloped off like mad and things were going very successfully while we were heading away from home. But on the return journey the donkey went faster and faster. Doug, running alongside, fell as he tried to keep up, I fell off the sleigh and Sansovino raced on towards the farm gates. Dad heard our shouts, came running out and tried to stop the donkey, but without success. She turned to go through the gates into the yard, the sleigh swung up into the air and hit the gateposts with a terrific crash, smashing them to pieces.

That was the last time we ever tried to put Sansovino into harness. But she was an incredible donkey, we all loved her very much and were absolutely horrified to be told one day that she had been sold inadvertently.

She was being looked after one winter at stables on a relative's farm and when we went to collect her in the spring she had gone. We never found out who had got her or what had happened to her, but we strongly suspected she was sold in a market for a few quid. It was a terrible blow to us all and I think there was quite a family row about it.

However, as the years rolled on, I entered more and more show-jumping contests, riding my father's horses or the pony Gladys, belonging to Charles and which had been passed down to me, or horses belonging to other people. I won literally hundreds of prizes as the best boy rider and rode in the horse shows at Olympia and Richmond to win a couple of medals.

Lots of people started to talk to my father about the possibility of me becoming a jockey, but he wouldn't hear of it. He knew the conditions some of the young apprentices had to put up with in different stables and he thought the life was too hard.

But when I was thirteen Miss Wilmot spoke to me about becoming a jockey just before the start of the Easter holidays and suggested that I might like to do some work with her horses at her Binfield stable. The idea thrilled me. She was a successful trainer with her sister, Mrs. Pym—as a woman, her licence had to be held in the name of her head lad, of course—and Gordon Richards had ridden a number of winners for her.

So on the first official day of the school holidays I got up at five o'clock, while everyone else was still asleep at home, and went over to Miss Wilmot's on my bicycle. It was a beautiful, sunny April morning and as I rode along the country lanes of Berkshire I felt on top of the world. By now, horse riding was my first and only love and seeing, working with and riding some of Miss Wilmot's fine thoroughbreds seemed the greatest prospect in the world.

I was in for a surprise.

3

The Start of It All

My entry into the world of horse racing was quite sensational. In less than a minute I was running like the devil to get out of it as fast as possible—but not running fast enough. Bang! I was flying through the air and landed on my backside with an almighty thump.

Miss Wilmot's goat was responsible.

When I arrived at her stables that first morning I rode through the gates into her stableyard, propped my bike against the fence and walked cheerfully and unconcernedly towards the head lad.

'What the devil do you want?' he asked.

I was about to explain, but he wouldn't listen. 'Get off with you. We can't have any kids mucking about here,' he said.

Obviously Miss Wilmot had not told him of the arrangement that I should work there during the holidays. I was about to argue when I saw the goat.

Many animals, understandably I suppose, like to have companionship and Miss Wilmot had this huge, well-built goat as company for some of her thoroughbred horses. It might have got on well with horses, but it didn't like strangers—particularly small boys who had obviously incurred the displeasure of the head lad.

It came for me with head lowered, so it seemed reasonable at that moment not to wait around and argue with the head lad as to why I was there. I turned round and fled, but Eph's short legs did not cover the ground quickly enough. If you have ever seen a goat in full cry you will know why.

Before I got anywhere near my bike it butted me full on target, and I took off unceremoniously in the direction of the main gate. Mind you, in those days I only weighed about five stone nine pounds, so the goat didn't have much opposition. I hit the ground pretty hard, but it did not seem propitious to worry about bruises at that stage with the goat poised for another charge and I was up again in a flash to grab my bicycle and get out of this madhouse.

Fortunately, at that moment Miss Wilmot came round the corner into the yard and in a second had taken charge of the situation. The goat quailed visibly at her explosive roar, allowed itself to be quickly tethered up and the head lad was told, in words of one syllable, that I had arrived there by arrangement to do some work.

This arrangement had been that I should work at Binfield Grove for just a few hours each morning, but I stayed there throughout the first day after Miss Wilmot had telephoned my mother to say where I was and for the rest of the holidays I continued to go there every day.

It was quite hard work but I seemed to thrive on it—rubbing down the horses, giving them their feed and doing other general work after riding out on her private gallops. It seemed certain that I was going to stay there and be taken on as an apprentice and I think Miss Wilmot wanted this to happen.

But then news of my new job reached the ears of a well-known Reading horse dealer Mr. Oliver Dixon, and he immediately contacted my father. He begged Dad to let me go to another trainer, the late Major Fred Sneyd, who had about twenty horses at his stables at East Manton, Sparsholt, Wantage. Mr. Dixon had two horses in training with the Major and pointed out to my father that I would be given a much better chance there than with Miss Wilmot's stable, where Gordon Richards naturally had the pick of the rides, had first retainer and was obviously quite certain to choose to ride anything which stood a chance of winning.

By now my father had become accustomed to the idea that I was determined to be a jockey and agreed that I ought to stand a better chance with the Major, who had a good reputation for bringing on young riders, was a qualified veterinary surgeon and was, apparently, anxious to have me.

It was decided I should go there, but I was not yet fourteen and the school authorities, still determined to try to make the Smiths toe the line, were not agreeable to my leaving. It was crazy, really, for the only tasks I had undertaken in my last few months at school had been to arrange different football fixtures with other schools in the area. Even so, the headmaster was adamant at first that I should stay on until the end of the summer term, and it was not until Major Sneyd guaranteed that I should have a tutor every afternoon that I was allowed to leave at the age of thirteen.

At last the great day arrived when my parents signed my indentures as an apprentice to the Major for what was supposed to be five years (but later, somehow, turned out to be seven), and I set off for Sparsholt, forty miles from home. I went in an open lorry, sitting on a bale of straw in the back while my father sat up front with the driver. Going away from home for the first time, it seemed like a journey of 500 miles and it wasn't long before I felt really homesick.

Eph riding the jumping donkey

(Sport & General)

Eph, as a young jockey, with Mr. Jack Jarvis after riding Ellenborough to win the Trial Selling Plate at Lincoln in March 1935

Eph falling on Beacon Bay at Newmarket in April 1936

(*Central Press*)

June 1938 and Eph rides Inscribe, trained by Basil Jarvis, to win the Churchill Stakes

I was supposed to be provided with clothing and equipment by the Major, but nothing had arrived when I got there and the only clothes I had for some time at Sparsholt were those I stood up in.

I was feeling decidedly low when I said goodbye to my father and despite the prospect of riding some fine horses and working with the animals I loved I felt like turning round and going back with him.

My feelings were not improved when I was shown to my quarters that evening, a converted wash-house at the back of the Major's house which was covered with cobwebs, had only an old paraffin stove for heating and was draughty and dank. I climbed into my bunk and crept beneath a solitary blanket wondering what had happened so suddenly to disperse all the wonderful aspirations and hopes I had had about being an apprentice jockey and what on earth had prompted me to leave the comfort of my home, my brothers and sister Gertie and the warmth of a happy family atmosphere which I had known all my life.

Frankly, my first-night fears were confirmed that Major Sneyd's place was really rough for young apprentices and, in fact, all the hands. The food was absolutely deplorable. For breakfast at 7 a.m., after we had already spent an hour getting the horses dressed down, putting on their tack and cleaning out the stables, the fare was a cold fried egg on a cold plate. Nothing else. Nor did we get anything more until about 2.30 p.m. when we had what was left after the Sneyds in the dining room, the servants in the kitchen and, I think, the dogs and cats, had all had their meal. Naturally, when this finally arrived it was dead cold too. At four o'clock we had a decent pot of tea with a margarine 'doorstep' and a piece of stale cake which you could generally bounce like a cricket ball on the floor.

Last meal of the day was at 8 p.m. when we had a bit of bread and cheese without anything to drink.

One day, after choking over the cold-fried-egg breakfast, I complained to the cook: 'Why can't we have something different and something a bit more filling?'

Unfortunately, Master Eph Smith was another Oliver Twist, I did not get any more and the only outcome of my complaint was that next day we were all given cold pickled herrings for breakfast!

I didn't complain again. But when my mother and father found out how bad the food was at Sneyd's they started sending food parcels to me and some of the other lads. But when Sneyd found out about this he stopped it on the grounds it would make us all overweight.

But Mum and Dad got round this by coming over as often as possible at weekends and taking us all out for a picnic. There wasn't much Sneyd could do about that.

The daily work started, after the alleged breakfast, with exercise and, having been brought up with horses, this was a bit more enjoyable. Then we would ride across the gallops or canter before taking the horses in, rubbing them down and getting the second lot ready to go out. Each lad had two horses to look after, including fellow apprentices Bobby Lightfoot and Frank Hunt and the board wageman.

When we returned and rubbed the horses down again we were ready for lunch, no matter what it was.

You might think we would get a bit of a break after this meal, but, oh no, the head lad set us to again in the afternoon, whitewashing the walls, cleaning out the boiler house, brushing down the yards or weeding the gravel driveway. And after tea it was back into the stables again to bed the horses down and if we were lucky we finished at about 6.30 p.m.

For this mighty effort I received a shilling a week for the

first year, three shillings a week for the next two years and five shillings a week for the two years after that. Believe it or not, when I was twenty and riding in something like thirty races a week I was still getting only ten shillings a week.

Eventually the only way I could make any spare pocket money was by fiddling on my expenses when I was supposed to travel by taxi through London to catch a connection to take me to one or other of the meetings in the South or East. When I first travelled to these meetings by train I dutifully followed Major Sneyd's instructions and caught a taxi from Paddington, where I would arrive from Didcot, to the next terminus for the train to, perhaps, Kempton, Sandown, Epsom or Hurst Park. But one day an apprentice from another stable told me about the Underground Tube service, how to get from Paddington to Waterloo, Charing Cross, Victoria or wherever it might be, and how to save my taxi fare in this way.

Instead of taking the five-bob cab across London it cost only sixpence on the Tube, and with the return journey to take into account, I could make nine-bob profit in a day like this.

It went very smoothly until one day Major Sneyd's car broke down and he said he would accompany me on the train for the meeting at Newmarket.

When we got to London he looked at his watch and said: 'Come along, Gordon'—I had been nicknamed Gordon in his yard from the day I started because I resembled Gordon Richards very much in stature—'come along, we have plenty of time for our connection at Liverpool Street. We'll catch the Underground Tube instead of taking a taxi.'

He led the way into the Underground station, bought the tickets and promptly marched straight along to the wrong platform. From my previous trips I knew very well that to get to Liverpool Street we ought to be catching the Inner Circle Line train, but, never supposed to have travelled on the Tube, I dare not say so. Sure enough, Major Sneyd got us on to the wrong train with me frantically wondering how I could break the news that we were getting further away from Liverpool Street every minute.

But I dare not speak up. Knowing his vivid Irish temper I feared the most tremendous roosting if I did, and it was some time—nearly at Notting Hill Gate, I think—before the Major discovered we were travelling west instead of east.

We hurriedly jumped off, caught a train going the right way at last, but arrived at Liverpool Street too late. The race special which we had been intending to catch had just pulled out. The Major was livid, for we then had to take a taxi all the way from London to Newmarket.

As we settled down for the long ride up the A10 he said: 'There you are, Gordon. Now you know why I've always told you to take a taxi in London. You never know where you are on these infernal Underground trains. Let this have been your first and last ride on them. Always take a taxi, my boy. Always take a taxi.'

'Yes, sir, yes, sir,' I said, all wide-eyed and innocent.

After that there was never any query on my London taxi expenses, whatever else might have been questioned!

But all this happened some time after I first started riding at race meetings and by then I had several winners under my belt.

During my first days as an apprentice all I could do was to listen and learn as much as I could and wait hopefully for the big day to come when I would be given a mount in a race. And as it turned out, I didn't have to wait long. It was only a month after I started that Major Sneyd called me into his big room and told me: 'Gordon, I have applied for your jockey's licence and I'm giving you a ride at Birmingham next week.'

I left him with my head in a whirl. I was just over fourteen, weighed under six stone and here I was going to race at a real meeting, against perhaps some of the most famous jockeys of all time, like Steve Donoghue and Gordon Richards, and with only the briefest knowledge of what conditions would be like when I got to the course itself.

Yet I was thrilled at the prospect. It seemed incredible that I should be taking this step less than two months after leaving school and, with the exception of Lester Piggott, I think it is probably still a record for a young lad to get a ride after such a short time as an apprentice.

Mr. Dixon had said that Major Sneyd was just the man for pushing on young apprentices and that he would give them every chance if they showed any promise at all, and in my childish dreams I vowed that I would do everything possible to justify the Major's confidence in me in giving me the Birmingham chance. Visions of winning or being placed fleeted through my young mind. This was to be the chance of a lifetime and I could barely sleep for thinking about it.

Yet on the day of the race I made a complete hash of the whole thing. I probably rode the worst race ever ridden by any young apprentice.

I finished tailed off last on the wrong side of the course.

4

'He'll Know Better Next Time'

IT was one of Major Sneyd's horses that I was to ride that day at Birmingham, an animal with a name I could hardly pronounce, let alone spell! It was called Chiaroscuro and was inclined to cross its legs and duck and dive while racing if you didn't keep it very steady. I had ridden it several times at home and felt I could manage it, but I did not take into account the practical considerations involved in racing itself.

To start with I had more butterflies in my stomach that day than any day before or since. Not even when riding Blue Peter in the Derby, almost ten years later to the day, did I have such taut muscles, such a dry mouth and such a weak-at-the-knees feeling.

I went into the dressing room and looked vaguely around until I bumped into Harry Yorke, who turned out to be my valet as well as Tommy Weston's.

'Come on, son,' he said kindly, and led me to a place where I could get into my racing silks. He showed me how to put my muffler round my neck and then led me to the trial scales to check that I was at the correct riding weight. He then put the necessary weights into my lead cloth, wrote out the chit telling my weight for the clerk of the scales and told me how to present myself in a few minutes to be officially weighed in front of the clerk.

Vaguely I remember putting the chit down on the

clerk's table, standing on the scales and receiving an 'O.K.' nod. Then I was outside, walking in a line of other jockeys to the paddock. I was completely oblivious to the crowds of smartly dressed men and women standing around the paddock or walking to and fro between the stands, or to the shouts of the bookmakers. I just spotted Major Sneyd, went straight over to him and stood with trembling knees as the head lad, 'Mac' McGregor, brought my horse over.

'. . . just try to get to the front, make the running and don't worry about anything else,' I vaguely heard the Major say.

I swallowed. 'Yes, sir.'

'Right then, up you get.'

Automatically I put my hands across the horse's neck, heaved myself up and, with a helping hand from the head lad, sat astride the horse. My feet fumbled for the stirrups. It seemed ages before they slipped in. Then the leathers were shortened, I had the reins in my hands and we were starting to move out.

I blinked, shook my head a little and with the horse between my knees, started to feel better and slightly more acclimatised as we moved off. When we got out on to the course I began to take stock of the surroundings, latched on to another rider and followed him all the way down to the start of the mile-and-a-quarter race. My mouth was still dry and my hands were sweating a little, so I rubbed them in turn on the legs of my riding breeches. I hadn't a clue whether anyone was betting on my horse but I hoped not.

It seemed we were at the start, having our names called getting ready to line up, before we had been there for more than a couple of seconds, although it was much longer, of course. I was drawn No. 6—not the best draw

—and looked around frantically to get in between horses Nos. 5 and 7 which would be on either side of me.

I watched as the starter climbed his rostrum, took a tighter hold of the reins and checked quickly that my feet were properly in the stirrups. We started to move forwards and I took a quick glance to the left to be sure I was roughly in line. The tapes seemed to come nearer and nearer and I prayed that my horse would not suddenly dive forward into them. I watched the starter again, suddenly saw his hand press down the starting lever, dug my heels into the horse's sides and, with a jerk, was off as the tapes swished to the top of their supports.

It was a good start and, remembering my orders, I went to the front. No one seemed to mind and I got my horse on to the rails, steadied him down and kept him going at a reasonable gallop. After a furlong I was three lengths clear, was starting to feel confident and was containing my horse nicely.

We pounded on, still with a useful lead, and I started to take the right-handed turn which would lead into the straight four furlongs from home. Still no one had come up with me and for one crazy moment I wondered if my wildest ambitions of winning on my first ride in public could be realised.

Then it happened. Behind me two or three horses had started to creep up to closer order and suddenly a fierce, rending shout almost made me jump out of the saddle.

'Get over. Pull out, son. Let me through.'

That was one jockey. Then other voices joined in from behind. 'Move over . . . for Christ's sake . . . get out of it . . .'

Like a fool I did as I was told. Almost round the bend, when I had the horse nicely balanced, I gave way. I thought it was the proper thing to do, I was so scared. Foolishly

I gave my horse a tweak and before I knew what was happening it had crossed its legs, swerved to the left and was ducking and diving across the course.

On my inside the other horses flashed past as I tried to straighten my animal up and get him balanced again. But he just would not have it. With me pulling like mad, he careered on until reaching the far rails where he started swerving from one side to the other as I tried to pull on him and get him steady. At last I did so, just in time to see the other horses slowing up and finishing the race with me still a hundred yards behind.

Back in the unsaddling enclosure Major Sneyd came across. His face was as black as thunder.

'What the hell did you think you were doing?' he roared.

I wished the ground could open and swallow me up. 'I'm sorry, sir,' was all I could mumble.

Sneyd was giving me a right rollicking when one of the other jockeys, Leslie Cordell, came across with a smile. 'Don't be too hard on him, Major,' he said. 'The other jockeys shouted at him to move over on the bend. He'll know better next time.'

The Major still glowered, but his tone was easier. 'Well, don't be such a damn fool again,' he said, and stalked off.

Nor was I. The lesson had been learned the hard way but I knew from then on that with a difficult horse like that you just could not try to take him out to let someone through on a bend when you had him nicely balanced. It was bound to lead to disaster.

But it was a very depressed Eph 'Gordon' Smith who arrived back at the stables that night. I couldn't sleep. I kept thinking about the race and what a fool I had been. It went over and over in my mind and I think I was still worrying about it when the head lad came in to wake us all up at six o'clock in the morning.

Would I ever get another ride? Had I ruined my chances before even starting properly? Had I cost the Major a lot of good face and spoiled his reputation for training apprentices? All these things flashed through my mind.

But Sneyd, for all his temper, was basically a fair man with his apprentices—when it came to riding, anyway. Later we had a terrible row because when my apprenticeship ended on my twenty-first birthday I found that the considerable sum of money I expected, and which should have been put by for me, was not as much as I thought it ought to have been. That was a long way off, however, and at that time all I knew was that even though he was a difficult man to please, he worked hard for his apprentices, taught them all he knew and was willing to help them along.

I think Sneyd must have known that, for the next few days after the disastrous first race I was moping around the yard, constantly wondering if I would ever get another ride, for it was not many days later when he called me in again and told me: 'I've got you down to ride at Alexandra Park next week. Good luck.'

That was all. I could have cried with relief.

It had come naturally to me to ride the thoroughbred racehorses at his stables when I joined. Having had so much experience in the show-jumping field there was not too much to learn. I have heard of apprentices starting at stables when they could hardly stop on a horse—and make good—but there were no riding problems for me. All I had to do was pull up the stirrup leathers and ride shorter with the knees up, in contrast to my former hunting style of riding long. The jaunty, streamlined riding style was introduced, I think, by Tod Sloane and caught on very quickly. In those days—1929—all the jockeys were riding this way and, of course, it helped a great deal in balancing the horse when galloping.

With my second ride everything went smoothly. I didn't win, I wasn't even placed, but the butterflies in my stomach were not so bad this time and I didn't do anything stupid. The Major seemed satisfied and by the end of that 1929 season I had had five more rides, all on horses he owned as well as trained, and although the nearest I came to being anywhere in the frame was fifth, I had learned some useful lessons.

The living conditions at the stables were no better, the food was still bad and on more than one occasion I thought about running away. Two other well-known jockeys, Eddie Larkin and Jimmy Lindley, who were apprenticed there after me, left because they could not stand the conditions and I can't say I blame them. But somehow I stuck it out, probably because I knew that with Major Sneyd I would have more rides than with any other trainer you could think of.

Part of the trouble with the Major was that he was always very hard up, at that time anyway, and but for two good friends of my father, Colonel Barker, Master of the Garth Hunt, and his huntsman, Mr. Daniels, I should not have had any riding breeches. They each bought me a pair from Bernard Wetherall's, the best you could get, and I wore them in turn day in and day out. I had to. I didn't have anything else.

It was not until I went on holiday—for my only week of the year—at Christmas that my parents realised that Major Sneyd was not kitting me out with decent clothes, as promised. When I returned after the holiday my father spoke to the Major about it and the next thing I knew he presented me with a new suit. It was the most frightful green colour, but it was quite good cloth, which was just as well, for it had to last me for several years. What would have happened if I had grown much more or put on very much weight I hate to think!

I've always been lucky with my weight, which is most fortunate, for it is a great worry to many top jockeys. It was a handicap for Charlie Smirke, Brownie Carslake, Stanley Wootton and others who lost many mounts because they could not get down to the lower margin, and Lester Piggott has trouble every year maintaining his usual riding weight.

Towards the start of the 1930 flat-racing season I had reached the incredible weight of six stone seven pounds (I don't know how it was done on the terrible food we had) and it was necessary to go light to ride at six stone two. I started to get the pounds off by running in heavy sweaters to perspire freely and was seen by one of the lads, Alf Sharples. He gave me some advice then which has served me well ever since.

'Look,' he said, 'you'll ruin yourself trying to sweat weight off in this way. All you will do is build yourself up, improve your muscles and make yourself grow. That's just what you don't want to do if you're going to stay as a jockey.'

His advice was to walk, walk and walk. It seemed a hopeless idea at first, but I took up walking, anything up to five or six miles a day, and, sure enough, down came my weight. From then on, even during the season when I wasn't travelling away to ride, I was given the afternoon off work in the stables to go for long walks. I was down to six stone two in no time and kept to that limit for some time.

Ever since then I have just walked away my extra

weight. In latter years I could ride at about seven stone nine quite comfortably. There was never any question of Turkish baths, sweat boxes, running in heavy sweaters, throwing things around in gymnasiums or doing any other wild exertions to get the extra pounds off. All I would have to do would be to start walking five, six, seven, eight, nine or even ten miles a day in the fields, on the roads and across the Newmarket Heath near my home, and from being perhaps eight stone six in January I would be down to normal riding weight in March.

Then, with reasonable dieting, such as having only a boiled egg and a cup of tea for breakfast, and fish or steak in the evening, I could remain at a steady weight for the rest of the season. I allowed myself to relax, eat well and drink pleasantly until January 1st each year and then, making a note of my weight in a diary, I'd start walking every day to be ready in time for the Lincolnshire meeting in March.

I feel sorry for jockeys who have serious weight troubles, particularly those who try everything possible to keep down to the upper-lightweight limits, but I am not so sorry for those who spend all their time in sweat boxes trying to reduce. I'm afraid a good many use only this method, the reason being they are too lazy to do anything else, such as taking long walks.

Ask any well-known jockey who doesn't have weight troubles how he manages to keep light and fit and he will tell you it is largely due to plenty of walking and no sweat boxes. Once you start on the latter method you will never be able to stay constantly at a reasonable weight.

I wish more young riders would take note of this.

We apprentices were supposed to be in bed by nine o'clock every night at Major Sneyd's, but now and again we used to creep out for a bit of fun in Wantage, four and a half miles away. One night I remember we all got dressed in the best things we had, climbed into bed, covered up and waited until the head lad had looked in (to make sure we were all there?), put out the light and gone away.

Then we slipped out quietly and walked to Wantage, calling to say hullo to a friendly neighbour, Mrs. Jenny Martin, on the way. She was always very sympathetic about our living conditions and gave us all a good meal before allowing us to set off again. At Wantage we went to a dance organised by a local hunt, where Gordon Richards and Freddie Fox were among the guests, and had a great time before setting off back.

When we reached the stables we froze in our tracks. A light was on in a box belonging to a horse called Hustler and we thought someone must be about. By this time it was 2 a.m. and we didn't know what to do. We could not risk being caught up fully dressed after 'lights out' for fear of getting extra work to do or of being punished, so we just had to lie doggo. The light stayed on continuously and we thought we would just have to wait until whoever it was decided to return to bed. The hours ticked by, nothing happened and finally, at about 3 a.m., one of us crept forward to see what was going on. Everything was quiet. There was no one about. We crept into our room and slid into bed as it was getting light, absolutely tired out.

When we discussed the matter in the morning we just could not understand why the light had been on all night in Hustler's box. At first we wondered if the horse had been 'got at' by dopers or nobblers.

Then we learned the truth. The Major's wife, Mrs. Marie Sneyd, had got some weird idea into her head that Hustler was afraid of the dark and shortly after our departure she had slipped outside to put the light on in the box.

We could have kicked ourselves when we heard that we had spent ages lying in the damp grass without sleep just because of a woman's whim that a horse was afraid of the dark!

However, despite odd incidents like this, the bad food and the hard work, in my second season with the Major things really began to look up from the racing point of view. More and more rides started to come in for me, and, at long last, on August 15, 1930, I had my first winner.

But in doing so I made that great jockey Gordon Richards very angry.

5

An Unexpected Victory

THE first of my 2,313 winners was a very game horse called Red Queen. It belonged to Mr. George Sneyd, surgeon brother of my boss, and, never having won a race previously, started at 20—1. In the same race Gordon Richards was riding a horse called Saragevo, strongly fancied by its stable to win and backed down to 5—2.

By now I had ridden in a number of races, there was no question of having butterflies in the stomach when going to the starting gate, and I was well acquainted with the routine of the line-up, race conditions and requirements. Being a five-furlong race, I knew it was essential to have a good start if I were to have any chance at all and my instructions were to jump off quickly, get to the front and, if possible, stay there.

It didn't work out like that at all. In the first ten seconds of the race I thought my chance had gone completely.

The field was a big one—fifteen or so runners—and since Red Queen was always a slow beginner it looked as if my chances had gone by the time I got going, for the leading horses were at least ten lengths away.

I cursed. Normally, in a five-furlong race you can have no chance without a good start. Missing out like that there was nothing I could do in the first furlong but to settle the horse down, get her nicely balanced, allow her to lob along behind the others and let her run her own race.

Windsor was the course nearest to my former home and

my family regarded it as a sort of local meeting. Dad was in the Silver Ring that day and told me after the race that as soon as he saw my bad start he thought I had made a mess of everything. He wasn't the only one.

But Red Queen had other ideas. To my complete surprise, after I had settled her down, she started to pick up the bit with just under three furlongs to go. Gordon Richards was well clear, about fifteen lengths in front of me at this stage, but gradually Red Queen started to close the gap. I passed one horse, another, then another and the further we travelled the faster my horse seemed to go.

With a furlong left I was still five lengths behind Gordon, who was riding his usual forceful race. But now I was in second place, and Red Queen almost flew the last 150 yards.

The champion jockey was still going fast, riding on a line about four yards from the rails, but as Red Queen was overhauling him with every stride I pushed her through on his inside. She kept going like a bird and strode in front almost on the line to win by a short head.

The crowd, which had naturally wanted Gordon to win and had been shouting him home, was hushed and shattered by this 'turn up for the book' and I rode to the winner's enclosure in almost complete silence. Not that I cared. I was overjoyed. I was far more excited than at any time before in my life and, looking back now, I realise that this was a moment of exaltation which exceeded that nearly ten years later when I won the Derby on Blue Peter. I could hardly get off Red Queen quickly enough to get on the scales, have my weight confirmed and hear those wonderful words which confirm a win without question: 'Weighed in'.

If I was completely happy at that time, Gordon Richards certainly was not. It had happened before and it has happened since that a young apprentice has beaten a senior jockey to record his first win and, while it has always been accepted with resignation, it does not make the pill any sweeter when it happens to the experienced rider. What had made it just that little bit worse in this case was that I had gone on the inside of Gordon's mount to get up and win, which might have been thought a bit cheeky. This, coupled with the fact that his stable had, apparently, had a bit of a gamble on the horse he was riding, did not please Gordon very much.

He gave me quite a roosting in the dressing room at first, but then Jackie Sirett, another of the jockeys, took my part and after a moment Gordon smiled and gave me a pat on the shoulder.

'You rode well. Good luck,' he said.

I mumbled 'Thank you, sir' and got changed feeling as tall as the grandstand at Epsom—and that's mighty tall for a little chap like me!

Among the people who rushed to congratulate me that day was my father and he had run into trouble trying to do so. He had gone into the Silver Ring instead of Tattersalls because, quite honestly, that was all he could afford to do, but when my horse was announced as the winner he could not contain his excitement. He ran out of his enclosure and raced along the course to get into the winner's enclosure, reserved for members only. Without thinking, he rushed through the gate, but the wary gatekeeper was very much awake. He put out his foot and Dad tripped over on to his face.

The gatemen were going to throw him out there and then, but someone in the enclosure recognised him just in time and shouted: 'His son's just ridden the winner, let him through; let him in.'

One of the gatemen nodded. 'O.K. We'll look the other way for a sec,' he said, kindly.

Dad was among the first to congratulate me and I think I was more pleased that he had seen the win than anyone.

While I was tickled pink to have won, I realised that it was a fluke that I had done so. Red Queen had run a number of times previously without doing anything, usually fading after four furlongs and finishing among the 'also rans'. But it didn't take us long to realise what had happened to cause the change.

As anyone who has ever had a bet on a supposed certainty and seen it go down the pan will know, horses cannot be relied upon to oblige by landing the odds. There are a number of reasons for this and one of them, which just cannot be fathomed, taken into account or relied upon in any way, is the temperament of race-horses. No matter how good a horse in any particular stable might be, he will have his own way of doing certain things and no power on earth can change the particular temperamental foible he may have. The only thing a trainer or a jockey can do is to find out as soon as possible what this foible is and allow for it.

Red Queen's particular temperamental streak was, quite clearly, that she did not like to be pushed to the front early in a race. Previous to her win she had always been started off quickly and pushed up with the leaders in the hope that she would stay a five-furlong trip. Apparently she did not like this idea at all. But when, as I've explained, I had that slow start, thought all was lost, and allowed her just to lob along, she got to liking the idea of having a race. Therefore, after a couple of furlongs, when she made up her mind to get going she grabbed the bit, strode out and went hell for leather.

Quite accidentally we had discovered the way she liked to race and under this different policy she turned out to be a very useful horse indeed, and she was always game as long as you let her take her time to get settled down.

My head was still in the clouds when I returned with Major Sneyd in his car to the stables that night. He had just said: 'Well done, lad,' immediately after my win, but that meant a great deal to me, for the Major was not famous for being very free with his compliments. It was a long time before I got to sleep that night, as I kept going over the race again and again in my mind.

For the subsequent few weeks things went very well for young Eph, still only fifteen, and by October I had had seventy-nine rides and seven winners. One or two of the newspapers were beginning to notice that I seemed to be a capable young jockey and had already 'written up' my defeat of Gordon Richards on Red Queen in the usual 'young 'un beats old 'un' sensational way. I used to chuckle about that. If they only knew the truth! But the other six wins were not flukes and, I suppose, deserved a mention.

As a matter of fact, some of the write-ups given to young jockeys in those days were quite out of proportion. I only discovered this on going through the newspaper clippings to write this book. Until then I had always thought that only the publicity given to young apprentices since the war was ridiculous and I blamed it for making some of the youngsters rather big-headed. Certainly there have been a number of young jockeys in latter years who have thought they knew all there was to know about riding racehorses when, in fact, it was about all they could do to hold the reins properly and stay on.

However, it seems that there has always been too much over-praise for young riders and it's a wonder that we didn't all get big-headed before the war. There can be only one explanation: we didn't read all the papers because we couldn't afford to buy them!

In my second season I was taken to a number of race meetings by Major Sneyd in his car. This was nice and comfortable but it had two disadvantages. First, it meant that I couldn't fiddle the taxi expenses as often as I would have liked; second, I kept getting a bath from the Major's dog which, apart from being decidedly unwelcome, was not particularly hygienic.

This Sealyham dog, called Sandy, used to sit in the back of the car between the Major and Mrs. Sneyd. I used to sit in front next to the chauffeur. A nice seat for me? Yes, it was—except that the big brute used to lean over the back of my seat, rest its head on my shoulder and in the stuffy atmosphere proceed to slobber all over me for the entire journey.

By the time I got to the racecourse my clothes were soaked. There was nothing I could do to avoid this slobbering, affectionate animal. If I moved over to the left, it came with me. If I pushed over to the right, the chauffeur gave me a dig in the ribs to get me off his arms and elbows. There seemed no solution, and I suffered a regular sousing.

Then the dog was stung by a bee. It happened in the yard at Sparsholt and the poor dog was very unhappy for a couple of days. But I noticed that for ever afterwards it avoided bees like the plague, which gave me an idea as to how I could avoid getting a soaking every time I travelled in the car.

On the next journey, as soon as we got going, the dog lolloped over the back of my seat as usual. And very quietly, out of the left-hand side of my mouth, I made a noise—just like a bee.

The dog leapt back and cowered on the floor.

A few minutes later it plucked up courage to lean over again, but before the first drip fell I started again.

'Bzzzzzzzzzzzzzzz.'

Down went the dog.

'Look out, Sandy, there's a bee in the car,' said Mrs. Sneyd.

'What? Where is it?' said the Major.

Everyone looked round, including me. 'It must have flown out of the window,' said Mrs. Sneyd.

The Major looked down on the floor, round the back of the seats and then patted the dog.

'All right, boy, stay down,' he said.

The dog stayed down . . . then and for ever more. If he made one move in my direction I gave a quiet buzz. It worked every time.

Towards the end of the 1930 season I was beginning to feel that my prospects of becoming a top-flight jockey were fairly good. I was winning the occasional race, riding with more confidence every day and getting to know a few more tricks of the trade. I was beginning to have rosy dreams of fame and fortune and, despite the poor conditions at the Major's stables, was grateful to him for giving me the chance of so many rides.

Then my whole world went tumbling over. Riding a horse called Noroc at Bath I fell. My leg was broken in two places, and in hospital six hours later through the mists of pain and semi-consciousness I heard a doctor expressing an opinion which would have meant the end of my riding days for good.

For he was saying to another doctor: 'I think we ought to amputate his leg.'

6

The Worst Hours of My Life

THE ten hours after my fall were the worst of my life. But for Mr. George Sneyd I don't suppose I should have ridden again. Being a leading surgeon as well as a race-horse owner and one of my favourite sponsors he knew how vital it was that my leg should not be amputated unless there was absolutely no alternative.

He took control of the case, called in orthopaedic specialists from London and persuaded everyone that there was a chance my leg would heal.

The accident happened about three furlongs from home in the Bath race. Noroc was never an easy horse to ride and had an inclination to hang towards the rails. It didn't have much chance of winning that day and when one of the jockeys started to overtake me his animal bumped mine quite accidentally. Noroc hit the rails hard and I was thrown over them. Unfortunately my left leg was caught in the stirrup iron and I was dragged along half on and half over the fence by the horse before the stirrup leather broke, I fell to the ground on the far side of the rails, and, thank goodness, the horse galloped on without me.

By the time I hit the ground I was almost unconscious. Someone ran across, took one look at my leg and said: 'Oh my God!' It was hardly surprising. The leg was bent at an angle and the shin bone was causing a bulge in my riding boot. When the ambulance arrived and they put me on a stretcher the leg flopped about like the end of a broken matchstick.

Major Sneyd asked me if I would rather go into hospital at Wantage or at Bath and I opted to go to the hospital nearest my home, even though Wantage was nearly fifty miles away. The ride there in the ambulance was so painful I almost wished I had stayed in Bath and I passed out several times on the way. It seemed to take hours to get there.

Inside the hospital it was ages before anything was done about my leg and I was constantly drifting between the conscious and the unconscious. One of the doctors must have thought I was 'out' all the time, for he held a bedside conference with another doctor and Mr. Sneyd and then suggested my leg should be amputated.

Mr. Sneyd would not have it. He said: 'For God's sake —he *is* a jockey, you know. What do you want to do? Ruin his life completely?'

X-rays showed that my leg was very badly splintered, but still Mr. Sneyd was adamant and insisted on calling in an orthopaedic specialist from London. He arrived that evening, shook his head a little doubtfully, but gave me a smile and said: 'Don't worry, young man, we'll soon fix you up.'

My leg was set under anaesthetic and the next thing I remember is waking up with it wrapped in plaster. But it was still there! It took ages to set and when, finally, the plaster came off after four months I realised how near it must have been to being amputated. There was a kink in it. In fact, there still is.

All the time in hospital I fretted to get out and ride again. The day after my fall Doug, who had also been apprenticed to Major Sneyd just before his fourteenth birthday—he is nearly two years younger than I—had his first ride in a race, and as I read the racing sections of the newspapers avidly I could see he was now getting a few more rides. So far he had not been very successful—he had to wait a year for his first winner, but I was very envious and kept thinking about the race meetings I was missing, the horses I should have been riding and the work I should have been doing. I couldn't wait to get back to the stables—tough as they were.

At last I was taken up to London where an iron was put on my leg and within a week, with this still on, I was back in the saddle. I had to take it fairly gingerly at first, but soon got my confidence back and was staggered to be told by Major Sneyd that he wanted me to ride Red Queen in the Portland Handicap at Doncaster. I was delighted to have the ride, but at that time it seemed ridiculous because I was still wearing the leg-iron.

But he insisted. I had a couple of gallops, still wearing the iron—it just tucked with my leg inside my boot—and although they went well I didn't feel that I was really ready to put everything into riding, should the need arise. And sure enough, it did!

In the Portland Handicap I let Red Queen run her usual idle race in the first stages and then, quite of her own accord and with only a little encouragement from me, she picked up the bit and flew the last two furlongs.

We overtook all but one horse called Xandover and although Red Queen was catching this one in the last 100 yards she didn't quite make it. We were beaten by a short head. It wasn't the horse's fault, it was mine. I just was not fit enough to put everything into driving her along those last few yards, otherwise there is no doubt she would have won.

Major Sneyd didn't say much about my losing the race. I had expected a roosting for not getting up to win, but, uncharacteristically, he was quite restrained. I think he realised that I was not fully fit and thought it better to say nothing.

On the other hand, he may have deliberately given me the ride with the intention of helping me to improve my confidence and if this was the reason I am grateful. Despite losing, I knew after the race that my leg was getting strong again, that my riding ability had not really been impaired and that next season I would be able to carry on just as though nothing had happened. It certainly worked out that way and I had ten winners in the 1931 season.

But it was not until 1932 that I really began to feel that my future as a jockey ought to be assured. It was confirmed, if anything, at the Epsom spring meeting when a bit of hard luck for Harry Wragg turned out to be a piece of good luck for me.

Harry, one of the finest jockeys of all time, whose judge of pace was superlative, could not do the weight for a horse called Roi de Paris in the Great Metropolitan Handicap at six stone seven pounds. The horse was an ugly type, small and grey, with a roughish coat and badly proportioned, and had been bought for only 175 guineas as a selling plater. It was trained by Douglas Pennant, of Upavon, Wiltshire, and never worked very well at home. However, he entered it in a seller at Newbury and to everyone's astonishment it turned out to be a real stayer and trotted in.

Hardly able to believe the good fortune, Mr. Pennant then entered it in the Great Met where it was very favourably handicapped.

Harry Wragg usually turned the scales at about eight stone one and could not possibly have ridden at this weight. He had always been most helpful to me, giving me advice about judging the pace of a race and how to wait on a horse until the precise moment to make a winning run—they called him the 'headwaiter' since he was so good at this—and when he decided that he could not ride Roi de Paris he suggested that I should be put up to ride instead. And he told me: 'I think it will win.'

It did. In the two-and-a-quarter mile race he settled down nicely near the front of the field and as we turned off the course to go over the track which, for three-quarters of a mile, serves as part of the course for this, the longest race at Epsom, it was obvious that he could stay the distance quite easily. Back on the course and rounding Tattenham Corner into the final straight, I pushed him to the front and he won in a canter. It was as easy as that.

In those days the Great Met was one of the most important handicaps of the year and I was elated to have my first big handicap winner. And as things turned out there is no doubt that this result had a marked effect on my future career.

Harry Wragg went on to prove that Roi de Paris really was a bargain horse when, at a weight which did not trouble either the horse or the jockey, they later won the Newbury Cup, another valuable handicap. Some seller that horse was! Meanwhile I had another good winner in a long-distance race, the Hwfa Williams Memorial Handicap, over two miles, at Sandown. I was riding a horse called Boldero and here again it was just a case of letting a good stayer settle down to outlast the others.

The bad luck which had already hit Harry Wragg in my favour struck again for the senior jockey much more seriously towards the end of the season. Quite simply, cantering down to the post and chatting to another jockey, he came a cropper when his horse stumbled. Poor

Harry suffered a broken leg and it put him out of action for several months.

The trainer by whom he was retained was Jack Jarvis, of Newmarket, and when he asked Harry if he had any views on who should ride for him until he was fit again he very boldly suggested me. It was not an easy thing for the experienced jockey to do, for I was still claiming an apprentice's allowance and, compared with him, was as green as the grass on Ascot race course.

But Mr. Jarvis decided to take the chance with me and I was invited to ride for him. He had some extremely good horses in his yard at Newmarket and it was a wonderful opportunity. I finished the last part of the season by getting more and more winners, and all told in 1932 had thirty-four.

So once again Harry's misfortune had been a landmark in my career. And it paid off in a big way soon after the start of the 1933 season when Major Sneyd called me into his office. 'I've got some good news for you,' he said.

I waited expectantly and he went on: 'Now don't let it go to your head and don't start getting big ideas. You've still got a lot to learn.'

'Yes, sir,' I mumbled, wondering what the heck it was all about.

The Major looked down at me, frowning slightly. 'Well,' he said, 'I think you can do it and I'm prepared to give you the chance. How would you like to go to Mr. Jarvis as his retained lightweight jockey?'

I could have danced a jig, but I told him: 'Oh, that would be very good, sir. I'd love it.'

He said: 'All right then. You can go. But understand, you're still retained by me as first jockey and if I want you and Mr. Jarvis wants you, then you will have to ride for me. I don't care if his horse is likely to win and I want you for a carthorse which doesn't stand a chance, you'll still have to ride for me.'

I nodded. 'Of course, sir.'

'Right. Off you go then.'

I walked out feeling about ten feet tall. What a chance! Only seventeen and here I was with a retainer to ride some of the best horses regularly from just about the best stable in the country. The Major only had about thirty horses in his yard at the time, none of which was particularly brilliant in class, and it seemed that only rarely would his horses and those of Mr. Jarvis run in the same race. And so it turned out.

For a seventeen-year-old I had a wonderful season. I had 561 rides and fifty-two winners. I rode Sans Peine to win the King Edward VII Stakes and the Goodwood Cup, a filly called Campanula to win the Windsor Castle Stakes and a horse called Apple Peel to take the West of Scotland Trial Handicap. They were all good races, particularly the Goodwood Cup, and it did my reputation no harm at all to be riding them into the winner's enclosure.

Sans Peine was a very good horse indeed, a nice bright bay, strong and a good stayer, but after winning the King Edward VII Stakes at a low weight he was not much fancied to win the big Goodwood race. Mr. Jarvis was keen on another horse he trained, called Foxhunter. Both horses were owned by Mr. Esmond and Foxhunter was undoubtedly the better of the two. Mr. Jarvis decided to run Sans Peine in the important race as a pacemaker for the other and engaged a very experienced jockey, Joe Childs, to ride Foxhunter, as Harry was still off with a broken leg. I was given very definite instructions to make all the running and did just as I was told.

I went out of the gate very smartly and took a three-length lead while Foxhunter stayed with the backmarkers.

As Sans Peine strode along in front I felt a little envious

of Joe, who I thought would be overtaking me about two furlongs from home, and I resigned myself to trying to keep my horse going and get a place. We turned into the straight after coasting smoothly down the hill and still I was in front. I couldn't hear anything breathing down my neck at that stage but felt it wouldn't be long before it did. But nothing happened.

I didn't know it until after the race, but Foxhunter had broken down just before entering the straight. He was tailing off last and I was on my own. Probably it was just as well I didn't know, otherwise I might have ridden differently and got beaten. As it was, with only two furlongs to go there was still no sign of Foxhunter pulling alongside me and I thought: He's leaving it rather late, I wonder when he's going to challenge?

A furlong to go and there was still no sign of the stable's No. 1 prospect and it hit me—at last—that something must be wrong with Foxhunter. I thought I had better pile on the pressure with Sans Peine, just in case. I rode him like mad and he turned out to be a better horse than anyone realised. He lengthened his stride, kept going like a train and, without anything else touching him, romped home at any price you like.

It was a nice consolation prize for Mr. Jarvis and Mr. Esmond, even if they were disappointed about Foxhunter. But the punters were not so pleased.

Several uncomplimentary remarks were shouted from the popular side as I rode Sans Peine in and one man shouted to the trainer and owner: 'You want to make up your minds which one's trying.'

Mr. Jarvis reddened and Mr. Esmond looked furious. I can only trust that if the shouting character had known how upset they both were about Foxhunter's breakdown he might have liked to bite his tongue off.

7

A New Employer

JACK JARVIS was a tough man for whom to ride. He had wonderful integrity, tremendous knowledge of horses and their capabilities and an understanding of races and racing which could not be bettered by any trainer in the country.

But at times he could show a hasty temper and if you got beaten on a horse which he fancied should have won, well, you had to stand by for fireworks. On the other hand, he would forget his anger as quickly as it rose and you generally knew exactly where you stood with him.

I always followed a trainer's instructions to the best of my ability even if I didn't always agree with him about the way the horse should be ridden in any particular race. But quite often, during a race itself, all the instructions would have to be thrown to the winds for a variety of reasons and you would have to make the best of things and still hope to win.

This happened many times with Mr. Jarvis and I was often roosted for not winning when I had apparently disobeyed instructions. But it is too easy to judge from the stands how a horse ought to have been ridden; it's not so easy when you are in the thick of it on the course.

For example, you may have to take the lead in a race much sooner than you really want to or have been told to. You may be nicely placed fourth or fifth, planning to make your run in perhaps another furlong, when suddenly all the horses in front start to weaken and you have to go through them or pass them in some way to avoid being completely hemmed in. It's no good sitting behind beaten horses when yours is still going well, because at the fateful moment when you want to get out and start your run you may be shut in so badly that by the time you do get out you've lost the race.

I have said that horses are temperamental and you cannot be sure from day to day how they will run. Nothing is more true and in just the same way no one can predict exactly how a race is going to be run.

Chubb Leach, the former trainer, once told me his view of the race-riding game which put the whole thing in a nutshell. He said:

'A good jockey doesn't need orders and a bad jockey cannot carry them out, so why give orders?'

I only wish more trainers would realise that.

I remember riding a horse for Mr. Jarvis called Hobo. It was a good horse with a nice turn of speed and Mr. Jarvis told me to ride a waiting race on him and come with a short, blistering run in the last furlong. I meant to do just that, but in the race, at Newmarket, I found that it was quite impossible for the other horses to match me at all and as we reached the dip I went to the front. I stayed there too, and trotted in an easy winner.

Mr. Jarvis, looking as pleased as if he had ridden it himself, said to me afterwards: 'You rode him a different way today then?'

I looked him straight in the eye and replied: 'Yes. He was going so well I had to.'

The Derby, 1939: Blue Peter lies third as the field rounds Tattenham Corner

The crowning moment in a career, and Eph smiles broadly as Lord Rosebery leads in Blue Peter after winning the Derby

(*Graphic Photo Union*)

Eph winning the Royal Hunt Cup in June 1946 on Friar's Fancy from Slide On

Eph on Full Dress (No. 5) winning the Woodcote Stakes in June 1949. J. Marshall on Radiant Hope (seen on the right) was second and K. Gethlin on Pennington (on the left of Full Dress) third

(*Fox Photos Ltd.*)

He just nodded and smiled again. But I dare not think what he would have said if my horse had been beaten.

The inescapable fact is that to be any good at all as a jockey you have to use your own judgment and think, win or lose, to hell with the consequences. As long as everything you have done has been reasonable in the best interests of the horse, the trainer and the owner, that you have tried your hardest to win and have played by the rules, then you can be satisfied in your own mind that you have done your best as far as circumstances permit.

Mind you, this is assuming that you have taken the elementary precautions of ensuring that your equipment is right, that you are fit in yourself to ride and that you know every inch of the course.

In my early days I always used to walk the course before going out to race on it for the first time. Even when I went over to ride in Ireland at the Curragh a few years ago I walked the course twice to make sure that I knew it well enough to give my mount every chance. I'm afraid a lot of young riders do not do that nowadays, hoping that everything will work out all right during the race. Needless to say, they have often found out to their cost that it does not.

One of the best horses I ever rode, but one of the most difficult, was Royal Charger, and he got me into trouble with Mr. Jarvis after a race at Newmarket shortly after the last war. He was a horse which had to be covered up until the last possible moment because he did not like racing alone in front. Before the race Mr. Jarvis told me that on no account was I to use the whip on him and to come on the stand rails. I disagreed with this view, thinking that most of the other horses would run down the centre of the course and that I ought to stay with them.

But Mr. Jarvis just said: 'Stay close to the rails—and don't use the stick.'

Roger Paris was the trainer's head lad and in the parade ring, as we were getting ready to move out, I leaned over to him and said:

'I don't think we shall win this one.'

Paris looked shocked. 'Come off it, Eph,' he said, 'you ought to be able to walk it.' He patted the horse and said: 'He's by far the best horse in the race.'

'I know,' I said, 'but the boss won't let me hit him and I've got to ride on the rails.'

He knew as well as I did that Royal Charger had to be held back and then given a couple of cracks with the whip to stir him up for a blistering final run.

It was a fairly small field. I was drawn on the stand side for the race and as anticipated after the 'off' all the runners went down the middle of the course, while I had to obey orders and stay on the rails.

Royal Charger, in blinkers, could only see immediately in front of him and as he was alone on the rails did not like the idea of apparently having nothing else to race with. He went well enough, even so, and a furlong from the winning post I had a quick look over my shoulder across the wide course and could see that he was only half a length behind the leader. Now was the time for Royal Charger to produce his final burst of speed. I wanted to hit him with the whip, just to give him a bit of urge, but I dare not disobey Mr. Jarvis after he had specifically said that this was not to be done. All I could do was dig my heels in hard, shake him up as best I could and ride him furiously with my hands.

It was not quite enough. I lost by a short head.

Back in the dressing room I waited for the inevitable

rollocking from Mr. Jarvis and, sure enough, in he came looking as black as thunder.

'Why the hell didn't you give him a smack?' he roared.

I said: 'You told me not to hit him.'

'Well, you could have waved your stick at him.'

I was really exasperated to hear this. For the first time in my life I answered a trainer back with a flash of temper myself. I shouted at him.

'What's the bloody good of waving a stick to a horse that's wearing blinkers?'

He looked absolutely thunderstruck. Then he turned, and without another word stalked out of the room. As his broad back disappeared through the door I almost wanted to run after him and apologise, but I couldn't. This was one time when I didn't see why the jockey should take all the blame for riding to orders and losing. But I thought the situation was pretty serious. No matter what the provocation, jockeys are not supposed to tell their bosses just how wrong they have been. They are like employees in any firm. If you disagree with the boss you don't do it forcibly. If you swear at him and tell him he's been in the wrong you can expect the sack.

That's what I thought would happen to me. I had visions of my £1,500-a-year retainer going down the drain and of being relegated to riding a load of rubbishy horses for a tatty stable.

I didn't see Mr. Jarvis again that day and had a disturbed night wondering what would happen next time we met. In the morning I jumped on my bicycle and rode out to Bury Hill on Newmarket Heath where I knew the Jarvis string of horses would be. I parked the bike against a tree and stood beneath the branches, watching, and wondering if I still had a job.

I saw the horses walking round and then noticed Mr. Jarvis speak to the head lad, who had already spotted me beneath the trees. He apparently asked Roger if he had seen me and I saw the head lad point to where I was standing.

Mr. Jarvis came across and, to my relief and astonishment, put his arm round me and said, 'Forget it, Eph.' That was all. It was enough.

It may not appear to have been a serious incident, nor one which I should have worried about too much, but in those days not even a senior jockey was expected to answer back when spoken to by the boss. Times are different now, but in the thirties and forties jockeys were still very much accustomed to discipline. It was tradition, really. As apprentices they had been brought up sternly by their bosses, always subject to the strictest discipline, and it became steeped in their minds that to obey was the absolute criterion. Any thoughts of rebellion could only lead to instant dismissal, a hiding or both, and it became second nature to take all the kicks without answering back. It might sound all rather Dickensian, but it happens to have been true. Jockeys never, never retaliated when spoken to sharply or unjustly criticised. They took it and suffered in silence.

I don't know if it was my answering back or the fact that I rode the same horse in 1945 to win the Newmarket Challenge Stakes, but next season my retainer was doubled to £3,000 a year. Then Royal Charger, covered up, ridden with the other horses and given a tap with the whip, went on to win the 1946 Ayr Gold Cup in easy fashion.

Yes, horses—and trainers—can be temperamental. Racing is always full of difficulties and uncertainties on both sides and we all have our problems, whether owners, trainers, jockeys, stewards, starters, bookies or punters.

Take the starters. Starting with the tapes has always been a dicey business, and I have seen jockeys hurt badly by a horse galloping into them. It's not always easy to line up in the right place either. A jockey usually finds his position in the draw in the starting line by checking on the position of the two horses which will be drawn on either side of him, unless, of course, he is drawn No. 1, when he will automatically be on the left. In this way, and with each jockey doing the same thing, it's not too difficult to get into the right order of the draw.

But sometimes you have to get in quickly and start in the wrong place. The starters are very fair and if they can't give you the chance to get into the correct position when they let the gate go, then they will not report you to the stewards. It is not very often you hear of a jockey getting fined for starting from the incorrect draw.

Before the war, when there were fewer runners and a twelve-horse race was considered a fairly big field, starting was not so difficult and it was not very often that you got 'left' at the start. If you did it was usually because you had an almost uncontrollable horse or were half asleep.

The big fields now, where there is often a lot of barging, pushing and shoving at the start—particularly for five-furlong races—are not really in the best interests of racing. They are not fair to owners, trainers or punters and I have seen many a hot favourite knocked out at the start of a race by being barged off balance at the crucial moment when the tapes go up. The starting stalls are a help now, otherwise all you can do is to try to keep out of trouble as much as possible, find yourself as much space as you can and plead with the other jockeys to keep their distance. You can also plead with the starter 'No, sir', 'Not yet, sir', 'Wait, sir' and so forth, but this doesn't do a great deal of good. If he sees the horses in line he lets them go—and that's that. It's up to the jockey to be on top of his job somehow and to get away properly. Of course, this doesn't matter too much in long-distance races, but in a five-, six- or seven-furlong race it is usually fatal not to get a good start.

Horses will quite often run differently for different jockeys. They will like the treatment of one and not another, simply I suppose because of the different styles and methods of riding. And they will quite often refuse to run as you think they should.

I once rode a horse called Honeyway and as a two-year-old he kept displeasing everyone connected with him by failing to stay even five furlongs. This was particularly upsetting, because he was bred well and should have stayed.

Two or three times I would get him off to a nice start and have a clear run for home, only to find that he didn't finish fast enough to win. Then, purely by chance, I was shut in soon after the start of his next race and no matter how hard I tried I couldn't get out until near the winning post. But I finished third, full of running.

Mr. Jarvis was ill at the time and I went back to Newmarket to tell him what had happened. Next time he told me to ride Honeyway from behind; the horse dropped nicely into the latter half of the field and, without being pushed very much, took hold of the bit after halfway and ran on to win a good race. In the same style he won the July Cup at Newmarket in 1945, and in 1946 the Victoria Cup at Hurst Park and the Cork and Orrery Stakes at Ascot.

In 1946 Mr. Jarvis decided to put him in the five-furlong Nunthorpe Stakes at York, but was very worried about being beaten by one horse, an Irish three-year-old called The Bug, which was supposed to be terribly fast. He thought by now Honeyway had had enough experience of racing to be able to run in any fashion and told me that, in view of The Bug's tremendous speed, it was vital to get a good start and stay with the leaders all the way, otherwise The Bug might slip him by several lengths and leave too many to make up.

But Honeyway had not forgotten his old quirk. I took him straight into the front from the start and sprinted for home, but after four furlongs he tired. I managed to keep him going, but another horse got up to win and I only finished second. And it wasn't The Bug that won, it was a horse called Golden Cloud.

We were all upset at this reverse, naturally, but came back for another race at Newmarket in which Golden Cloud was also entered. This time I rode Honeyway from behind and, sure enough, he came through with a terrific finish to beat Golden Cloud quite easily into second place.

I was so impressed with the way he was going at the end that I told Mr. Jarvis I thought he could now win a longer race, say a mile and a quarter, and Honeyway was entered in the Champion Stakes at Newmarket. I must have been left by ten lengths at the start when another horse crossed me, but Honeyway still got up to win easily at the finish. He had got so used to making his own pace by now that he was then entered in a mile and a half race at Thirsk. And what a race that was!

By now all the other jockeys had cottoned on to the way Honeyway wanted to run and held back from the start to try to make me go on in front. But my horse wouldn't have it and went slower and slower. He just dropped his bit and went jogging along behind until about two furlongs from home when I shook him up and he cantered to an easy win. He was certainly one of the most intelligent horses I ever rode. But not the best by a long way. That accolade must go to Blue Peter.

8

'We Will Win the Derby'

IN the spring of 1938 when I arrived one day to ride for Jack Jarvis at his stables at Park Lodge, Newmarket, I could see that Mr. Jarvis was looking pleased. His voice was cheerful, he walked with a jaunty step and he greeted me pleasantly.

'Good morning, Eph.'

It was just before the start of the racing season, when he would normally have plenty to worry about. We exchanged pleasantries and then he said:

'Eph, I want you to come and have a look at one of my two-year-olds.'

He took me across to where a number of horses were being walked round and pointed to a nice-looking well-grown, obviously backward horse which was a chestnut.

'There. What do you think of him?' asked Mr. Jarvis.

I watched the horse walk round and noticed that he moved easily and was very, very calm and placid. I nodded: 'He looks extremely nice. What's his breeding?' I asked.

Mr. Jarvis told me he was classically bred by Fairway out of Fancy Free and was owned by Lord Rosebery. 'We call him Blue Peter,' he added.

He didn't say any more, except 'keep an eye on him',

but I could tell he liked the look of the animal very much. However, I was kept busy during the next few months, riding out in the mornings and racing six days a week, sometimes in every race of each day, and I forgot all about Blue Peter until later in the season. Then Mr. Jarvis told me I would be riding him in the Imperial Produce Stakes at Kempton Park over six furlongs and I remembered that this was the animal he had so liked the look of at the start of the season. However, by this time the boss had a horse he also fancied very much called Admiral's Walk, but I still thought it would pay dividends to ride Blue Peter.

In that first race at Kempton I wanted to give Blue Peter an easy introduction to racing and took him along very carefully. If he could have won without being pushed too hard I would obviously have let him, but it was essential not to knock him about at all and get him to like the idea of racing. He was easy to manage and finished third, with Admiral's Walk taking second place.

I was well satisfied with his performance, particularly the way he had settled down nicely and accelerated when I shook him up just a little at the end, and I told Mr. Jarvis that Blue Peter showed great promise. Mr. Jarvis then wired Lord Rosebery—'We will win the Derby.'

He had one more race before the end of the season and showed even more promise, finishing second to Casanova, a horse trained by Captain Cecil Boyd-Rochfort. He was not very far behind, I didn't push him too hard and it was a successful result because Blue Peter was still backward and Casanova was thought to be pretty useful.

Blue Peter was then let down at the end of the season and after doing well during the winter came out as a nice, strong colt with a beautiful action. I started to ride work on him over five furlongs. He worked with Old Reliance, who the previous year had won the Ayr Gold Cup with me as a three-year-old, and worked every bit as well as him. Then Mr. Jarvis put him to work over a mile with a horse called Agincourt who the previous year had finished fourth in the Cambridgeshire carrying seven stone twelve pounds. But Agincourt could not stay with Blue Peter and we began to realise that we had a horse on our hands that was something really special.

Blue Peter's first race of the season was not until April when he was entered in the Blue Riband Trial at Epsom. He remained as placid as ever on the course and won the mile and 110 yards race quite comfortably, this time putting behind him Boyd-Rochfort's horse Casanova.

Six days later he won the 2,000 Guineas at Newmarket, giving me my first Classic winner. Admiral's Walk was second. Blue Peter was always going well and, to my mind, there was never any doubt about the result. Coming out of the dip when I met the hill he lengthened his stride and from sixth position swept by the others to win by a length quite easily.

He was immediately made favourite for the Derby and I thought this was absolutely justified. But not in any race so far had he been really pushed and I told my solicitor, the late Mr. Tom Stutchbury, that Blue Peter would not only win the Derby but the St. Leger as well. I wrote him a letter saying: 'The only danger to Blue Peter in the St. Leger is Hitler.' How right, unhappily, this forecast turned out to be.

After his Guineas success Mr. Jarvis started to train Blue Peter for the Derby distance of a mile and a half. He was worked with a number of other useful horses, but always finished these gallops full of himself and with what I call a 'double-handful' left in him.

Then came the day when Mr. Jarvis decided to let him

really go all out and it resulted in a tremendous row after what at first appeared to be a serious set-back.

Mr. Jarvis's instructions were that in this Derby trial gallop I should let him stride out the last two furlongs after going round the turn near the paddock on Newmarket Heath. There were several good horses in the trial with him, and, to watch the trial, Mr. Jarvis stationed himself on his hack, about two furlongs from the end of the gallop.

We set off at a good gallop and with just over two furlongs to go I went to the front, took a length's lead and, to my amazement, found that Blue Peter would not go any further ahead, no matter how hard I tried to push him. Then, as we approached Mr. Jarvis, he came across on his hack in front of us, turned it alongside me and, cursing me, he started to gallop like mad. I suppose he must have been as disappointed as I was that the colt had not left the other horses behind by more than a length, for I had been telling him how good Blue Peter was and how well he had been going in previous gallops.

Anyway, I finished the gallop only just in front of Mr. Jarvis's hack and he immediately told me to go and wait for him in his office. He gave me another blast to send me on my way and I was feeling really depressed.

In the office I found Lord Rosebery and I quickly told him what had happened. After all, it was his horse and I thought he was entitled to know.

He said: 'Well, never mind, Smith. But whatever Mr. Jarvis says to you don't retaliate. I think it was a good gallop.'

When Mr. Jarvis came in he still looked furious, but he didn't say too much more and I drove away in my car feeling very down-hearted. Then in the centre of Newmarket I met Mr. Robert Jewett, whose father had trained a great horse in its day called Isinglass, and who was assisting Mr. Jarvis.

And I was astonished to see his eyes gleaming. 'My word, Eph,' he said, 'that was a great gallop Blue Peter did this morning.'

I looked at him as if he were daft. 'What do you mean? I thought it was bloody awful,' I said.

He looked quite blank. 'You're joking. Don't you know how far you left those others behind when Mr. Jarvis jumped in with his horse?'

It was my turn to look blank and I asked him what on earth he was talking about.

And he explained. As soon as Mr. Jarvis had ridden across in front of me to give me a rocket Blue Peter had lengthened his stride and gone after Mr. Jarvis's hack.

Said Mr. Jewett: 'Your horse must have made up half a furlong in the last two furlongs. He left the others way behind.'

I could have kicked myself for not noticing. But with Mr. Jarvis's wrath to contend with I suppose it was not surprising and I began to realise just what an outstanding horse Blue Peter was.

In that trial, and left far behind, had been horses which included Admiral's Walk and another called Tutor which, as a three-year-old, had won the Manchester November Handicap by six lengths.

I wiped my brow. 'That's a relief. I wondered what had gone wrong. Blue Peter must have accelerated so smoothly I didn't notice,' I told Mr. Jewett.

The explanation was now clear about our Derby prospect. He would do just enough to get comfortably in front and would then do only enough to stay in front. He was a bit lazy and not until we saw another horse ahead did he want to do any more.

I went back to my lodgings with kindly Mrs. Sanderson feeling very much better and, after breakfast, flew off to York for a couple of unsuccessful rides. Then I flew back to London for the Derby Dinner as Lord Rosebery's guest and during the interval he took me aside for a chat.

He said: 'You know, Smith, Mr. Jarvis didn't realise this morning how far you had left all those other horses behind. He is perfectly satisfied with the gallop now.'

I have told you how Blue Peter won the Derby so easily and there is no doubt that that Derby week was my lucky week. The morning after the big race I heard that one of the hunters I had been riding the previous day, Fair Orb, was going to be bought for £1,000 by George Beeby, the trainer, as a potential chaser.

For me, 1939 was a great season altogether until, as I had forecast, Hitler intervened to rob Blue Peter of the chance of winning the Triple Crown.

Very few horses in history have won the Guineas, Derby and St. Leger and it was a great shame that he did not have the chance to run in the Leger. It is as certain as anything can be in horse racing that he would have won. There was absolutely no doubt about his ability to stay the mile and three-quarters of the Leger course and, as the quiet, cold war turned out in 1939 when hardly a shot was fired, the race could quite easily have been run.

However, before the war stopped all racing for a while after September 3, Blue Peter won the Eclipse Stakes at Sandown, and in a gallop before this race Mr. Jarvis put him in with a four-year-old called Challenge, which had finished second in the St. Leger the previous year. It was a very good horse indeed. Doug rode him in the gallop and I was giving him about five pounds, but Blue Peter finished alongside him with a 'double handful', which was a great effort for a three-year-old.

In the Eclipse itself Blue Peter did not appear to run quite so impressively. Unknown to me, he had cast himself in his box a couple of weeks before the race and, although he was fit in time to run, he was short of work. About a furlong and a half from home at Sandown he had gone to the front and then, with the crowd cheering him home, he started to doddle. To my horror a horse ridden by Bobby Jones started to challenge and I heard the crowd's cheers turn to an angry roar. But I knew Blue Peter could still win and just riding him with my hands and feet he got home by three-quarters of a length.

There was a lot of criticism about how he had only just won, but what no one noticed was what happened just past the winning post. When I went to pull Blue Peter up I could not at first and he went round the top turn as if the devil were after him, passing the starter, the late Major Robertson, coming the other way. In fact I nearly cannoned into the Major's car.

Blue Peter was full of stamina. Ten days before the Leger should have been run we galloped him over a mile and six furlongs with three- and four-year-olds, including Flyon, which had won the Ascot Gold Cup. He finished as strongly with Flyon as in every other gallop.

Undoubtedly, Blue Peter was one of the best horses ever. I am only sorry he never had the chance to prove it, for after the St. Leger Lord Rosebery had planned to keep him in training as a four-year-old. It's difficult to say now how he would have compared with Sea Bird II, Santa Claus, Royal Palace, Pinza and other famous post-war Derby winners, but I am sure he was as good as, if not better than, any of them. He was certainly the best horse I ever rode, and out of 18,000-odd rides, that's saying quite a lot.

9

Personal Affairs

It was in 1936 that I had attained my freedom—in two ways—on coming 'of age' at twenty-one, as they say, and at the same time finishing my long, long apprenticeship with Major Sneyd.

Never was freedom more appreciated.

Major Sneyd had always done his best to put me in the top ranks of the jockeys. He had given me plenty of rides, plenty of encouragment, plenty of good advice and, through arranging my retainer as lightweight jockey with Mr. Jarvis in 1933, had put me firmly on the road to success.

But there were two unfortunate matters which had upset our relationship. The first concerned the length of my apprenticeship and the second concerned the amount of money due to me when I finally reached the age of twenty-one.

It had always been understood during the first years of my apprenticeship that I had signed on for five years, meaning that by the time I reached nineteen I should have been on my own to choose for myself for whom I rode. But after about three years Major Sneyd said that my apprenticeship would last for seven years and produced an agreement concerning my apprenticeship articles which confirmed that my father had signed for this. We tried to

(*Sport & General*)

Left to right: Doug, Charles, and Eph Smith at the Hawthorn Hill Open Coursing Meeting in December 1945

Eph on his pony, Peter

(*R. Anscomb*)

Eph riding Mr. J. V. Rank's Strathspey to win the 1949 Cesarewitch at Newmarket

Riding Premonition to win the St. Leger, 1953

argue about it, but there was not much we could do. Quite honestly, I don't suppose my dad had read the agreement properly in signing it in the first place.

The second item, concerning the money I felt was due, was rather more serious. By the time I reached the age of twenty-one I had ridden 215 winners and had had over 2,300 rides. As an apprentice I was supposed to receive half the money for these rides, plus half of the owners' ten per cent presents for winning. It was to be held in care for me by the Major and should have added up to several thousand pounds I thought.

But to my horror I received only about £1,000 and, unfortunately, it meant that solicitors had to be brought in. There was never a very satisfactory outcome and I won't dwell on the subject, but one of the things I did do was to buy my brother Doug out of his apprenticeship with the Major when he was nineteen, and what a good thing I did!

Doug was already proving to be a remarkable jockey and even before the end of his first 'free' season had made enough to pay back to me the money I had loaned him to be released from his apprenticeship. As many people will know, he went on to become champion jockey five times after the war, something which I was never quite able to do, and is still considered by many people to be the finest British jockey we have, ranked only with Lester Piggott.

Before 1936 I had ridden the winners of several big races, including the Manchester November Handicap on Pip Emma in 1934, the Lincolnshire Handicap on Flamenco in 1935 (the first of my three Lincoln wins), the Cesarewitch on Near Relation (also 1935) and the Welsh Derby on Bideford Bay.

As soon as I left Major Sneyd I signed for Lord Rosebery and Mr. Jarvis's stable as No. 1 jockey. It was an association with them which lasted fifteen years, until Lord Rosebery, who had not been having the best of luck with his horses, decided that a change of jockey would not come amiss and my good friend Bill Rickaby became his first jockey. I then joined Mr. H. J. Joel, first with the late Jack Watts—father of the present trainer of the same name—as trainer and then under Ted Leader, and I stayed with them until I decided to retire at the end of the 1965 season.

From 1936 until Blue Peter's year, as I call 1939, I had 272 winners, 1938 being my best year, with 114. Among them were the winners of the Scottish Derby on Faerie Queen (1938), the Victoria Cup on Phakos (1938) and the Ascot Gold Vase and Goodwood Cup on Fearless Fox (1937).

In 1939, by the time racing was curtailed on the advent of war, I had ridden seventy winners, including, of course, the 2,000 Guineas and the Derby.

As soon as war started, I endeavoured to join up, but my hearing trouble, which had gradually been getting worse, resulted in my being graded C3 and they just would not have me. At first, when I went for my medical examination, I think the examiners thought I was trying to pull a fast one by saying I could not hear everything that was said to me, but the chairman of the draft board knew me personally and told me that it was not purely in my own interests that I was to be graded C3.

'You might get other soldiers into difficulties at a crucial time by mishearing or not hearing an order,' he said.

So I went back to riding work for the first few weeks of the war and early in 1940—February 5, in fact—I married Doreen at a very quiet ceremony at Dullingham, near Newmarket, and we settled down in a house I had bought in Snailwell Road, Newmarket, in the early part of 1939 (a lot of people thought the house was a present given to me when I won the Derby, but as a matter of fact it was not!), and we have since lived there very happily with our three children, Robin, Neil and Erica.

Snailwell Road, on the outskirts of Newmarket, is one which has strong associations with racing. Living next door was Willie Pratt, the trainer who did so well in France before the war, and other residents before and since have included the late Miss Dorothy Paget, the controversial owner, my brother Doug, the Queen's jockey Stan Clayton, Tommy Lowrey, Fred Lane and Fred Archer. Next door is the Equine Research Station. My home, Meynell House, was, in fact, the former home of trainer Tom Waugh.

Neither of my sons has shown much interest in riding, although Robin, the eldest, graduated in 1967 as a veterinary surgeon at Edinburgh University. Neil obtained a B.A. degree in modern languages at St. Catharine's College, Cambridge. However, daughter Erica, having obtained 'A' level passes in languages at school, likes riding very much and I hope will go on to take an interest in show jumping and hunting.

Incidentally, it is very strange these days how the female sex always seems to predominate in show jumping. I can't think of any reason for it, but I do know that before the war it would have been considered most odd for the ladies to be the premier riders in this sphere.

Doreen is the daughter of a colourful character who was called Elijah Moore. He combined farming with bookmaking and had started his turf commission agent's business in a pub called the Three Tuns, which in those days stood at the Rookery, Newmarket. Then he moved to another pub, the Bull Hotel, before opening an office in Kingston Passage.

He was eighty-six when he died and sport had been his

life. He followed cricket, boxing, athletics and horse racing, but his greatest love was shooting, at which he was sensationally good. In 1911 he won the Monte Carlo Grand Prix for live-pigeon shooting, the last Englishman to win this, the blue riband of the pigeon-shooting world, and to compete in other shooting events he travelled all over the world.

He was untouchable and won many extravagant wagers through his prowess. A plaque commemorating his Grand Prix win is still placed on the shooting ground behind the Casino, not far from that of Tod Sloan, who had won the same event in 1908.

Elijah had a son and three daughters, Doreen being the youngest. Her sister Iris is the wife of Tommy Lowrey, the jockey who rode Airborne to win the first post-war Derby in 1946.

It was Elijah who started my interest in shooting in 1940 and he was therefore partly responsible for the development of my other hobby, the training of gun dogs. The other man responsible was Mr. R. W. Colling, father of trainer Jack Colling.

It was quite some time after taking it up before I became really interested in shooting, and I was doing so badly one day at Six Mile Bottom, near Newmarket, that Mr. Colling turned to me and said: 'You'll never be able to shoot unless you have your own dog.'

And without further ado he presented me with a light-brown Labrador pup called Scaltback Dan.

Dan turned out to be an absolutely superhuman dog and became famous for miles around. He would retrieve anything—darts from a dart-board, bottles on the floor, books in their shelves, playing cards from the table and even children from trouble spots. At least, he retrieved my elder son Robin three times when he was a youngster.

The first time it happened was when my wife was out and I was supposed to be looking after the little lad. For a minute I turned round to look at something in the garden and when I looked up again Robin had disappeared.

I had horrible visions of him getting out of the garden on to the road for a moment, and shouted: 'Robin.'

Without a moment's hesitation the dog bounded off into an herbaceous border at the side of the house and emerged a moment later with the boy firmly gripped by the seat of his rompers.

On two other occasions the dog saved Robin from a rather ferocious cow we kept at that time. The boy had toddled up to this cow in the paddock and when I looked across it seemed as if the cow were going to butt him. Again I shouted 'Robin' and the dog went to collect him by the seat of his pants.

The second time he was retrieved from the cow was when I was demonstrating the dog's prowess to a friend. I let him wander across to the beast this time and, when he got close, just called his name. Sure enough, the dog rushed over to retrieve him.

Nearly every time when people visited us Dan would have to perform his retrieving tricks and one particular admirer was Gordon Richards. He was a fairly frequent visitor to tea in his riding days and never failed to ask for a demonstration from the dog.

Out shooting with the veterinary surgeon Mr. Fred Day, and perhaps Mr. H. J. Joel, the dog would work like a trojan and never seemed to miss picking up a bird or spotting where it had landed in half the time it took other dogs to do the same.

One very cold day we had shot a partridge near Six Mile Bottom, Newmarket, and no end of hunting would reveal where it had fallen. We decided to call it a day, and started for home, but Dan would not leave the area. We had walked for over quarter of a mile when suddenly the dog appeared, carrying the partridge in his mouth. He had been determined to find it, but, in doing so, had become very exhausted.

I had terrible thoughts of him becoming ill, so pulled out my brandy flask and gave him a large swig, which caused him to have a good shake and a tremble, but fixed him up perfectly. He wasn't ill, anyway.

Sad to say, however, Dan got out of the garden one night—in search of a bit of romance, I believe—and somehow got on to the railway line just outside Newmarket and was killed.

Mr. Fred Day says that Dan was so good, however, that he spoiled me for other dogs because I expect too much from them. Perhaps I do, but it's still a very satisfactory hobby and perhaps one day I'll find another nearly like him, if not quite as good.

We mourned him for ages, but he started off my love of Labradors and I have trained a good few since then.

In fact, my interest in dog breeding often resulted in friendships being started with people which, happily, still last today. Chesney Allen, who used to lead the Crazy Gang, came to tea, and Bud Flanagan bought a dog from me.

Bud and Ches, by the way, gave me one of my most embarrassing moments when I went to see them at the Victoria Palace. It was their habit to pick out any celebrities in the audience and play a diabolical trick on them.

The night I went they found out somehow I had booked and had the seats for Doreen and myself switched to the very front row of the orchestra stalls. Soon after the show started Bud ran on to the stage with a pole which was about ten feet long, climbed down the steps to the stalls and as he reached me suddenly shoved the pole in my hands and said: 'Hold on to this.'

Like an ass, I grabbed it, and he turned and ran back on the stage.

I was left, literally, holding the pole. I couldn't put it down anywhere, it was too big. I could hardly pick it up, it was so heavy, and I just had to sit there with red cheeks, feeling the biggest nit in the world, while the audience roared with laughter.

Every few seconds Bud would turn, stare down at me and say 'Keep holding it' or 'You won't drop it, will you?' and I just had to sit there and take it until, at last, one of the attendants came and took it away.

My shooting hobby has also resulted in my making a lot of good friends and getting some most enjoyable outings with people in or connected with racing. Some of the best days have been shooting with the owners or stewards of the Jockey Club, including Lord Rosebery, the Duke of Norfolk, Lord Willoughby de Broke, Sir Donald Buchanan, Mr. Jim Joel, Mr. Stanhope Joel and other well-known figures in racing, and I have always felt it quite an honour that the farmer's son from Berkshire should be twice invited to shoot in such exalted company as the Jockey Club.

10

War Years

THE war years were difficult for everyone, of course, but some people connected with horse racing had a very tough time of it economically. With so many meetings cancelled, fewer owners and consequently fewer horses in training, the trainers particularly found it difficult to make ends meet. I don't know how some trainers managed to survive with the overheads on their property, which had to be kept up, plus the problems of being understaffed and overworked.

When I was turned down for the Army I became an ambulance driver, but some rather nasty-minded persons did not appear to know this, for I twice received white feathers in the post.

Of course, the people who send these things anonymously are to be despised, particularly when they haven't even bothered to find out the facts, and I did not take them too seriously. But they were upsetting for my wife and I remember that our postman, who knew the family and the true circumstances, was in tears when he had to deliver them.

They were stuck to postcards, which had been posted in Newmarket, and as he handed the first of them over the postman said: 'I'm terribly sorry, Mr. Smith. I hate to deliver this. I asked the postmaster if I could burn it or throw it away but he said I couldn't because it was the law that all letters and cards should be delivered.'

He really was upset and I felt much more sorry for him than I ever did for myself, although I wouldn't mind getting my hands on the person who sent them, even today!

As an ambulance driver I arranged to be able to work at night so that I could keep up my riding during the day.

Most of the other jockeys were in the Forces and, of course, when there was any racing I had plenty of rides. The difficulty was getting to the courses to ride them.

If the meetings were at Newmarket no travelling problems were created for me, but if they were either at Salisbury, or somewhere up north, jockeys and trainers would have to spend hours and hours travelling on cold trains, often without food, to get to a meeting. Sometimes four or five of us from Newmarket would pool our valuable petrol coupons to go by car to a meeting, but, more often than not, it seemed we would have to go by train or cadge lifts.

I remember one of the people who used to give me lifts from the race course at Salisbury to the station, a distance of four miles or so, was the late comedian, at the top of his fame during the war, Vic Oliver. He was an extremely nice man and I always wished he had had more luck with the horses he owned.

I was always glad of his lifts, for I often had to walk all the way from Salisbury Station to the course.

Another thoughtful person was Bill Bentley, who ran the Oyster Bar in London's Swallow Street. Quite often he would stay open after six at night, the usual closing time in those days, so that some of us jockeys could have a meal when we were crossing over London on our way back to Newmarket after a meeting in the South somewhere. There were not many oysters in those days, but he always managed to rustle us up a good meal of some kind.

I should have ridden the winner of the 1944 wartime Derby at Newmarket. It was partly my own fault that I didn't ride Ocean Swell to win and partly a mix-up about rides. The reason I did not ride Ocean Swell was because I thought that another horse would beat it—a horse called Growing Confidence.

This horse was one of the first Classic products of Blue Peter and ever since he was a yearling I had had my eye on him, and for sentimental reasons I naturally wanted to ride anything which came from Blue Peter's strain. Ocean Swell was also by Blue Peter, but he ran such a terrible race in the 2,000 Guineas I did not think he had any chance. Anyway, I was so wrapped up in Growing Confidence and I wanted so much to ride Blue Peter's first Classic winner that I told Lord Rosebery about him. Growing Confidence was trained by George Beeby and I got permission to ride him in the Derby instead of riding Ocean Swell. Lord Rosebery readily agreed to release me, knowing, I think, of my tremendous enthusiasm for anything connected with Blue Peter. He thus engaged Willie Nevett, who had ridden Ocean Swell in the 2,000 Guineas, to ride him in the Derby.

I was therefore surprised and horrified when I rang up Mr. Beeby to find out that another jockey, Ken Mullins, had just been engaged to ride Growing Confidence in the Derby. I thought it was a rotten thing to happen, particularly as I had earlier helped to school this son of Blue Peter. In fact, I had ridden him for hours round country lanes and through quiet areas, because he was not too happy at first in a string of horses.

Mr. Jarvis was surprised to hear that I wasn't going to

ride Growing Confidence after all, but thoughtfully fixed up for me to ride the Aga Khan's horse Tehran.

This was a very-well-thought-of colt and in the big race came third. Actually, I think Tehran could have won the race and beaten Ocean Swell but for a row between two stable boys a fortnight before the Derby.

These two boys had been squabbling over something when we were out on the gallops and decided to be little knights without armour and bore into each other with their horses while on the gallops.

Unfortunately, when they decided to do this I was riding Tehran in between them and they struck into my horse. He suffered a bruised leg as a result of it all and had to rest. It meant he lost his last gallops before the big race and was not fully prepared. Another few training outings would have made all the difference, for he came third to Ocean Swell when not fully fit. Even so, Willie Nevett rode a good race on Ocean Swell and we would have been very pushed to have beaten him.

Growing Confidence finished behind me in the field, so I wouldn't have won on that.

It just goes to show—no matter how good you think you are as a jockey and how much you think you know—you don't know everything. It's always helped to realise that.

After the Derby I rode Ocean Swell, as Mr. Jarvis's first jockey, in the Column Produce Stakes at Newmarket. It was a three-horse race with my two opponents being Tehran and a lightweight put in as Tehran's pacemaker.

This time Tehran was really fit and, having ridden him in the Derby, I knew I was going to have my work cut out to beat him. Mr. Jarvis had instructed me to sit on Tehran's heels until the last 100 yards from home and I did just that. But as soon as I challenged Tehran quickened beautifully and held me off to win by a head.

The Derby form had been reversed. But there was one thing I had noticed during the last seconds of the race, and this was that Tehran obviously liked to have another horse to race with. Many horses are like that and if you can spot it your chances of beating them are much improved.

Therefore, when the two animals met again in 1945 in the Ascot Gold Cup I decided to ride a different race on Ocean Swell. Mr. Jarvis was not at the meeting that day, because he was unwell, and I could only hope that I would be doing the correct thing.

I rode the race from behind again, keeping just astern of Tehran, and when we turned into the straight there were only two horses in it—Tehran and Ocean Swell.

Tehran was racing close to the rails and instead of trying to go up alongside him I pulled out into the centre of the course. This meant that I was racing alone, but it also meant that Tehran was too—and he didn't like this at all. I won quite easily, or, at least, much easier than I would have done had Tehran had my horse to race with alongside him. Having won the Gold Cup in 1939 on Flyon, I was more than satisfied.

Ocean Swell and Tehran were both damn good horses, really, and I wouldn't like to say which of them was the better. I just recall that it was a pity Tehran wasn't fitter for the Derby, as he and Ocean Swell would then have had a great race.

In the years 1940–5 I rode a total of 280 winners out of 1,800 rides, but not until 1946 did racing really get back into its full stride again. Then I had one of my best-ever seasons, riding 112 winners, including Friar's Fancy in the Royal Hunt Cup and the Victoria Cup on Honeyway.

My best-ever year was in 1947, when I rode 114 winners —only sixteen less than Lester Piggott had to win the championship in 1965—and for a long time looked like achieving my ambition of being champion jockey, until Gordon Richards pipped me on the post.

My departure from the Jarvis stables at the end of the following year, when I again rode 112 winners, was a big wrench. I had always found Mr. Jarvis an extremely good trainer, fair, and a good man to work for. We had our occasional verbal battles, but they were never very serious, and we would forget an argument had even happened within a few hours. Even though I was not retained at his stables I still rode for him many more times.

11

Outside of Racing

I HAVE always been very hard of hearing. In fact, since the last war I have been completely deaf and have always had to wear a hearing aid.

First signs of deafness showed up when I was a little boy and the family used to sit around the old wireless set with a cat's whisker and take it in turns to listen to the B.B.C. on the headphones. The trouble was that when it came to my turn I could never hear anything, although everyone else could.

The treatment? I was taken to the doctor, examined and, believe it or not, was put into hospital to have my tonsils and adenoids out. Not surprisingly, there was no improvement and ever since I have been getting more and more deaf.

In the post-war years without the hearing aid I could not have heard a thing. And riding had not been made any easier before then through being unable to hear just how close other horses were getting to me if I happened to be leading in a race. So something had to be done, as my hearing grew worse, and a hearing aid was suggested.

To start with I had a set which had a huge weighty battery attachment. I used to wear this thing until after I had been given my orders in the paddock and then take it off and hand it to the head lad to look after for me until I got back.

Eventually a much smaller dry-cell-battery instrument was brought out and I found I was able to wear this even when riding. The two tiny batteries fitted into a little container which I had in a sort of holster beneath my racing silks and the wire used to trail from there to the pick-up behind my ear, held in place by a springy band across the top of my head.

It always enabled me to hear just enough of what was going on in a race. But when I first wore it on full volume I had the fright of my life. It wasn't adjusted properly and the galloping horses sounded more like a herd of buffalo in a stampede. The only trouble was that even with this on people used to have to speak loudly at me and, like all deaf people, when I speak to others I do so rather loudly. It didn't matter at home, when I was with friends or relatives or when I was with trainers and owners I knew well, but it did matter sometimes.

I have always been regarded as rather an outspoken person, calling a spade a spade, if you like, and my forthright opinions have not always been welcomed by owners, particularly when I have been asked to tell them what I think of their horses.

Quite honestly, in recent years, some of the horses in training have been absolutely useless and it has been my misfortune, like so many jockeys, to have had to ride some of them. Consequently there have been big fields leading to much interference and rough riding, and good horses have had their chances ruined.

If I happened to be on a really bad horse and was asked by its owner after a race why it had not done better I used to tell him. I'd say 'He's a bad horse' or 'I don't think he's got any guts for racing.'

These remarks might have been all right and the owners might not have been much offended if I had spoken in low tones, but, as I told you, I always spoke loudly. And I can now understand an owner feeling somewhat disconcerted to be told in a public place in stentorian tones that his horse was, virtually, no bloody good.

Mind you, only a low percentage of owners were ever really offended. Most of them welcomed the advice, whether it was palatable or not, and took steps accordingly to decide what to do about the animal's future.

Indirectly, therefore, you might say that my outspokenness has cost me a friend or two, but if this has been the case these few people have been outnumbered ten to one by the people who have been helpful: jockeys, trainers, owners, stable lads, and, very important, starters, who have made plenty of gestures to help me understand exactly what they wanted done.

Being deaf has had its disadvantages but it has also had its advantages in that I have always had to use my eyes as much as possible in a race to make up for not being able to hear anything. Consequently, I always seem to be seeing things that other people don't see. In one race at Lincoln, a two-mile event at an evening meeting, I was making the running. It was nearly dark and for some reason or other all the officials on the course had gone home with the exception of the stewards, the starter and the judge.

Only a small crowd remained. There should have been people around the course to make sure that nobody got in the way, but, incredibly, they had decided to take an early night off.

We were going along quite smoothly and I was in front when I was staggered to see approaching me a boy on a bicycle. It was a racing cycle, I remember, and the boy had his head well down over the handlebars. We were all heading towards him at a steady gallop and when he looked up to see the horses approaching him in full sail he just fell off his bicycle with fright. He went over right in front of us. All the other jockeys in the race were watching me and thank goodness my eyesight was working well that night. I pulled out just in time to swerve past him and the other jockeys followed me. If any of us had gone over that bicycle I would hate to think what the consequences would have been, not only for the boy but for all those who were riding close behind me. When we got back to the dressing room the jockeys said: 'Thank goodness you were looking where you were going, Eph. If we had run into him it would have been like a battlefield.'

A lot of people were upset when it was decided to close the Lincoln course, but it was not a tragedy to me. It was always a very cold and miserable place, particularly at the start of the racing season, and with so much open common land and so many people able to wander on to the course at any time it was always liable to be hazardous. Without rails to follow it was a difficult job for the jockeys to make sure they kept on the course and we were not sorry to ride there for the last time.

The second time my eyesight saved disaster was at Alexandra Park. On this occasion I rounded the bend with about four furlongs to go, only to see an ambulance man and his stretcher across the course right in front of us. I yelled and pulled out and although it was at the turn we all just managed to miss him. Anyone in front who had had his head down would undoubtedly have hit this fellow and knocked him for six. He might have had good use for his stretcher, but so, unfortunately, would a number of the jockeys as well. How he got to be on the course in that position, at that time, heaven only knows, but I know he certainly got a roosting from his superiors for being in the way while racing was going on.

The third incident concerning my eyesight was at Hurst Park. Again I was making the pace in a race over a mile-and-a-quarter and as we turned into the straight I was horrified to see right in front of us one of the ramrods which are used by the course attendants to knock down the horses' hoof-marks in the grass on the course. This ramrod was standing up and it looked as if we were going to run right into it. None of the other jockeys, they told me afterwards, had seen this thing sticking up and again it was my keen eyesight that had prevented an accident. I swerved outside it, the others followed me and again we just managed to avoid trouble.

In each of these three instances it will be seen that I was riding in front at the time the incidents happened, but I never really enjoyed leading the field. Sometimes it is necessary to do so because you are on a horse which is an out-and-out stayer and the only way you can win is by wearing down the other horses through setting a strong pace.

I always preferred to come from behind and, although a lot of racing people seem to think otherwise, this has always been the method I have adopted whenever possible. Apart from anything else, racing is much more exciting if you can ride that way.

If I have been lucky with my friends I have never been lucky with the holidays abroad I have chosen, except the last overseas trip to South Africa, with my wife, when we were entertained by Fred Rickaby and his wife.

Up to then the holidays had always seemed to end in disaster. On one trip, to St. Moritz, it started all wrong when I found my passport was out of date at Calais and I only got into France under sufferance. Then, after I had been learning to ski for less than a week, a guide took me to the top of the 'professional' ski slopes on the ski lift. I'm never very keen on heights and halfway up to the top of this mountain my guide fell off his half of the drag lift and, being a lightweight, I was left dangling on the other side. At the top I tried going down the slope gingerly and gently but kept getting up to a terrific speed, so frightening in fact that the only way to stop was to crash. I quickly lost a ski this way and was so fed up I said 'To hell with it all' and walked the rest of the way back to the hotel. It was a long way, a terrific strain on the back of the legs and took four hours.

Another year we went to Monte Carlo, where it's supposed to be nice and sunny in the winter, and it snowed every day. We went to Malta for another holiday where the climate is nearly always fine, and it rained all the time and anyway we didn't get on with the drinking water. Another year I went to Marrakesh, North Africa, with my friend Walter Wisher when I was still recovering from jaundice. I don't know if I still looked a yellow colour but the Arabs kept staring at me madly and frightened the life out of me.

That did it. From then on, apart from the South African trip, we settled for Torquay or Bournemouth.

The only trouble with having a holiday in England has been that a number of people—certainly not all, by any means—seemed to want to get to know us just because I happened to be a jockey. I don't know whether they thought I was going to keep them in clover for the rest of their lives with winning tips, but if that's what they did think they were unlucky. Apart from the fact that I never tip winners, and if you know you are on a horse that ought to win it's not a matter for you but for the owner and the trainer if they want to impart any information about it, betting is an extremely hazardous business.

There is no such thing as a racing certainty. Horses are

so temperamental, so many things can happen in a race to upset the chances of an alleged 'cert' and a hundred and one things can go wrong, that betting and tipping by jockeys is a highly dangerous and expensive pastime. It's not allowed, anyway, although everyone knows that certain jockeys do it.

I've known jockeys who have bet on their horses when they looked sure to win getting into a hell of a tizzy during the race because things did not go quite as had been planned. They've been penned in and unable to get out, beaten on the run-in by a horse they knew nothing much about or which had not shown its best form previously, or they've been on a horse which, like Oncidium in the 1964 Derby, ought to have skated the race but decided for some unearthly reason it didn't want to know that day.

I've even heard of a horse which ought to have won refusing to race at all because it had been stung by a bee at the start.

As far as I can see there is no need for jockeys to bet anyway. Some of them do have a hard time of it, but can usually make a reasonable living by riding plenty of work if they want to. The others, in the top flight, as they say, should not need to bet. They get seven guineas a ride these days, win or lose, and ten per cent of the prize money in decent races when they win. They should make very decent money, and do. Why risk chucking it away?

12

Royal Jockey

I HAVE always been regarded, so I'm told, as being as much a horseman as a jockey in the 'top ten'. When I say 'horseman' I mean that there is a slight difference between him and someone who is purely regarded as a jockey; someone who has probably been brought up with horses and has spent his life working with them and who has a real affinity with them.

I was always supposed to have good hands and a delicate touch and I think this was in my favour when I was asked to ride Her Majesty the Queen's horse Aureole.

As a two-year-old Aureole had always been a difficult horse to ride. He always pulled hard and, with a soft mouth, caused himself no end of pain with his antics.

I first rode for the Royal Family in May 1950, when Captain Boyd-Rochfort asked me to ride Above Board in the Yorkshire Oaks. She was then owned by His Majesty King George VI, who, quite honestly, had some rather indifferent horses at this time.

However, Above Board was not one of the indifferent ones and when I won on her in the Yorkshire Oaks I was asked to ride her in the Cesarewitch at Newmarket that same year. Harry Carr, who was normally the King's jockey, was unable to do the weight on her in this race, which was hard luck for him but good luck for me. For

Above Board was a very good filly. She stayed well and had a very good turn of speed and won the Cesarewitch quite easily.

I started a new trend among jockeys when I asked King George VI to give me a pair of cuff-links instead of a tie-pin after I had won for him on Above Board. The late Captain Moore, who was the King's racing manager, was a bit surprised to receive my request, but I told him I had never much cared for tie-pins and I thought the cuff-links would be much more suitable anyway. He went to the King, discussed the question with him and a few weeks later my cuff-links arrived. From then on all the other jockeys who rode for the King received the same kind of present, as well as the usual percentage for the winning ride.

The cuff-links are among my most treasured possessions, along with a silver cigarette box which I received from the Queen after I had won later on Aureole. The box is engraved 'Elizabeth R'.

It was the third time I had won the Cesarewitch, having won the previous year on Strathspey for the late Mr. J. V. Rank and Near Relation in 1935. My fourth win in the race was in 1961 on Avons Pride, owned by the late Major L. B. Holliday.

It was three years after Above Board's win when I was riding at a Kempton Park meeting that Captain Moore, the Queen's racing manager, asked me if I would ride Her Majesty's horse Aureole in the Cumberland Lodge Stakes at Ascot. Harry Carr again could not do the weight.

Just previously I had at last won the St. Leger on Premonition for Captain Boyd-Rochfort, having been placed nine times in this Classic from 1936 to 1952. Premonition was not one of the 'great' Leger winners, but he was a useful animal and ought to have won the Arc de Triomphe in France in the same year. In this top French Classic race he was cantering as we entered the straight and I thought he had every chance when one of the French riders—they are not always courteous over there—either decided I looked a likely winner or thought he ought to put me out of action for some other reason. Anyway, everything looked set for me to win when suddenly this French horse struck into me. Even then Premonition went on for another half a furlong before collapsing completely. I pulled him up and found that his leg had been badly struck into. He had the most enormous gash in his offside hind leg and I was afraid he might have to be destroyed. However, very careful nursing by Captain Boyd-Rochfort saved his leg and he was eventually able to race and win again.

Aureole had run in Premonition's Leger and finished third, and although this may sound ridiculous, I hesitated before accepting the chance to ride for the Queen. I can almost hear people asking, 'How could anyone not jump at such an honour?', and of course it was a great honour to be given the invitation. On the other hand, I didn't want to make a mess of things in the royal colours, so instead of saying 'Yes' straight away I told Captain Moore that I would just like to ride Aureole at work as he was reputedly 'rather a handful'. I wanted to make sure that I could control him properly and ride him decently before I went out on him in public.

When I first took the horse out on Newmarket Heath I asked Captain Boyd-Rochfort to put a neck strap on him so that I could put my fingers in this rather than be constantly pulling on the reins and tearing at his mouth. He went much more kindly ridden like this and I decided to take the ride on him at Ascot.

When I went past the clerk of the scales at Ascot the clerk, Mr. Charles Manning, saw me with the neck strap and said: 'A lifeline eh, Eph?'

I laughed: 'I hope so.'

Well, a lifeline it turned out to be. Aureole won by about a length and a half quite easily without having a hard race and it was clear that he preferred the neck strap.

At the end of the 1953 season Captain Moore asked me if I would accept a retainer to ride for the Queen the following season, and I felt it was a very great honour to be asked to give Her Majesty first claim on my services. But I had to turn it down.

My mind was in a turmoil for a few minutes and then I realised what my decision would have to be. I had already agreed to be retained again by Mr. Joel and having done so there was really no question of changing my mind. Mr. Joel was not only a very good owner with some nice horses but he had always been extremely kind to me. Quite obviously my first allegiance was to him, but it was a wonderful gesture by Her Majesty to ask me to ride for her.

I told Captain Moore my decision and he must have gone back and spoken to the Queen about it. For soon afterwards he asked me if I would agree to a retainer to ride Aureole in all his races next season. This seemed a likely prospect, as Mr. Joel did not have any horses which would often, if ever, clash in races with Aureole and I said that if Mr. Joel had no objection I would be delighted to do so.

Sure enough, Mr. Joel agreed to the request and I had a wonderful season with Aureole. The first time I rode him as a four-year-old he finished second at Sandown, rather unluckily, as my horse was badly interfered with just turning into the straight. But he went on to win the

Coronation Cup at Epsom in a canter and he then won the Hardwicke Stakes at Ascot.

Before this race Aureole had had a slight accident with one of his legs and there was some doubt as to whether he would run. However, Captain Boyd-Rochfort got him sound and he was left in.

Just before the Hardwicke Stakes I had a conversation with the Queen, which, as it turned out, became an amusing legend in the horse-racing world.

Her Majesty was chatting to Captain Boyd-Rochfort when I arrived in the parade ring to ride. Unknown to me, Aureole had hurt one of his eyes slightly in a bump in the horse box on the way to the course and the Queen had just been told about it.

So after I had touched my cap and bowed she said to me: 'What bad luck, Smith.'

I thought she must have been talking about the horse having hurt its leg. And I replied, 'Oh, he's sound enough now, ma'am.'

The Queen said: 'Oh no, I didn't mean his leg. I meant his eye. He bumped his eye coming along in the box today and he can't see out of it.'

I just could not resist saying: 'Well, ma'am, we're both handicapped then.'

She looked rather puzzled: 'Oh! Why?'

'Well,' I said. 'He's blind and I'm deaf. Our chances can't be too good, can they?'

Captain Boyd-Rochfort looked rather shocked at my boldness for a moment, but Her Majesty laughed.

Anyway, Aureole won the race, and quite an eventful one it was too. In the last furlong I was in front until the late Manny Mercer—a wonderful man and a really great jockey, whose death later in a fall at Ascot was a tremendous tragedy and a blow to racing—drew alongside me on a French horse trained for M. Boussac by the former British jockey Charlie Elliott.

Manny was riding very close to me, in fact you could barely have separated our horses with a slip of paper, and I was horrified to see that he was gradually gaining a slight lead. Aureole had put his ears back at being challenged so closely and looked as though he was going to 'pack it in' and give up the race.

There was only one thing to do and that was to give him a crack with my stick and shake him up that way. It worked splendidly and Aureole started to shoot forward again. For several yards Manny and I raced side by side, still almost tied together, and Manny's quite legitimate tactics of challenging so closely rebounded on him a little. He had his whip in his right hand but with his horse beautifully balanced for the challenge he could not change hands to use his whip with the left hand—and being so close he could not use it effectively with his right. I had the advantage over him in that I'd been able to give Aureole a crack and in the last few strides we just got in front to win by a short head.

Manny was a bit upset at not having been able to use his whip and when we pulled up he said to me: 'I'm going to object to you for interfering with my use of the whip.'

Several people in the crowd on the popular 'Heath' side overheard his remark and started to boo, because a win for the Queen was obviously a popular one.

I shook my head at him. 'You can't object, Manny. You were riding too close,' I said. And added: 'Anyway, you can't object to the Queen.'

By the time we had got back to the enclosure he had cooled off a bit and, like the good chap he was, realised that what had happened was no one's fault. He said no more about an objection.

Michael Beary, the former jockey whom I always thought was the best horseman of all the jockeys, said that I was made for Aureole, which was such a difficult horse, and he agreed with my father's old saying about the way horses should be treated.

He had always told me: 'Imagine that the bit in a horse's mouth is a piece of silk.' In other words, use it delicately and never try to force the bit upon a horse. That was the way Aureole liked to be ridden.

But no matter how delicate I tried to be with him he was almost always indelicate in his response. In the King George VI and Queen Elizabeth Stakes, the richest race at that time, with a £27,500 prize, he started to play up in the parade in front of the stands and rather than go farther down the course, as we should have done, I turned round and started to go towards the starting gate before the parade was over.

But then, as we got to the starting gate, a man in the crowd suddenly put up his umbrella, causing Aureole to shy and leap a few feet into the air. Jockey Smith was propelled likewise and finished up on his backside on the lush Ascot turf. More often than not when a jockey is thrown off near the start his horse decides to take full advantage of this unexpected freedom and make a break for it. But Aureole must have felt guilty about tossing me off so unceremoniously, and instead of running off, decided that it was preferable to have a taste of some of the delightful-looking turf and meandered across to the rails near the start to do so.

When riding him at work I had always given him a handful of grass to promote friendly relations, so this time I picked up a chunk of Ascot's best, walked across to him with my hand held out and said, 'Come on, old man.'

Surprise, surprise! He took the grass and I grabbed his reins quickly and jumped on his back.

The troubles, however, were not yet over. When the starting gate went up, Aureole dug his toes in for a moment and we were left ten lengths. Luckily, the field did not get off to a very fast pace and I was able to take my time about catching up without too much effort. I moved into a handy position at Swinley Bottom, was going well in about third place turning into the straight and took up the running about two furlongs from home. I thought it was going to be fairly easy until one of the French challengers, Vamos, tried to get on terms with about a furlong to go. However, I remembered the race with Manny Mercer, picked up the whip and gave Aureole a tap—only the second time I had ever touched him—and he produced a brilliant turn of speed to hold off Vamos and win by three-quarters of a length.

The Queen was delighted. It was a really great effort on the part of her horse to win such a valuable race, particularly after such setbacks, and I was more than relieved to dismount, at last, in the winner's enclosure.

The Queen was a gracious and charming owner to ride for and was always terribly thrilled when one of her horses was successful in a race, particularly if the race happened to be run at Ascot. And I well remember one occasion when I rode her horse Snow Cat to win there that she was overjoyed. After I had dismounted she excitedly proffered her hand for me to shake.

There cannot be many people in the world who have refused to shake hands with a member of the Royal Family, but I did that day.

It is strictly against the rules for a jockey to touch anyone until he has weighed in after a race, so at that moment I had no alternative but to refuse to shake hands with Her Majesty. I don't suppose anyone would have said anything much if I had, but I thought it was better to be safe—just in case.

It was terribly embarrassing to have to do so, but when I said, 'I'm sorry, ma'am', shook my head slightly and touched my cap, she quickly withdrew her hand and said: 'Oh, of course not.'

She smiled and added: 'Anyway, well done, Smith. You rode a wonderful race,' and it all ended quite happily.

13

Trouble with Television

THE most extraordinary things can happen on race courses and when I say there is no such thing as a racing certainty I really mean it. For example, in a two-horse race you can generally reckon that one animal is red-hot favourite because it justifiably has the better form, while the other animal might be at any price.

Well, the idea of making a horse odds-on favourite in a two-horse race is, to my mind, very silly. The odds can easily be upset.

I remember riding a horse called Mermaid in a two-horse race at Ascot, the other horse, a red-hot favourite, being ridden by the champion jockey Gordon Richards. In the race neither of us wanted to make the running and when the starting gate went up we both sat still. The crowd booed and finally the starter yelled at us, 'Get going.' Being hard of hearing probably helped here, because the starter's roar must have sounded much more ferocious to Gordon than it did to me. Anyway, he started off first, but only at a walk and when he had gone a few paces I walked off too. Then we started to trot, but the crowd booed again. I think they felt they might be there watching us for the rest of the afternoon, for it was a two-mile race! However, I was determined to stay in second place for as long as necessary, for I knew that my horse was as good as

Gordon's over a shorter distance, whereas in a longer race, properly run, she was hardly in the same class. Going off first, Gordon had no option but to make the running, but by the time we were racing properly, the two-mile event had virtually been cut to less than half a mile. In the last furlong I was able to get in front and stay there to win.

Both Gordon and I came in for a lot of criticism about the way the race had been run and not only from those who had backed the hot favourite. Some racing correspondents wrote articles which really upset me, and my solicitor took it up with one of them. However, he wrote a letter of apology and I decided to let it go at that.

But it just goes to show—you can never bet safely in a two-horse race because it's likely that it may not be properly run.

Nowadays jockeys have to face another hazard in racing: the television cameras. Not only do these cameras spotlight the riding from close in for most of the race but they also have microphones at various parts of the course and around the enclosures to provide racing sound effects as a background to the commentaries.

When racing was first televised I landed in trouble with the stewards. Of all things, I was told off for swearing!

The incident happened at Sandown Park in a race which was being televised. I remember I was riding a horse for Mrs. Lambton which stood a good chance of winning, until Lester Piggott, quite innocently I must admit, interfered with me. Anyway, by the time I had got out of trouble it was too late to do much about winning and I finished fourth.

After I had pulled up and started to ride back to the unsaddling enclosure I found myself alongside Lester. And as we turned into the drive which goes off the course to lead behind the stands at Sandown I turned to Lester to give him a few well-chosen words for interfering with me.

'What the —— —— did you do a —— —— thing like that for?' I yelled.

Being deaf, as I've said, I talk louder than most people and this yell at poor Lester must have sounded like a clarion call.

Anyway, a few days later I was called over by Major-General Sir Randle Fielden, one of the stewards, who said: 'Smith, please be careful what you say on the course these days.'

I blushed a bit, remembering that I often used a colourful phrase or two and wondered where he could have been to have heard me. So I was horrified when he added: 'Every word you said to Piggott came over on the TV.'

I don't think I have sworn out loud at a televised race meeting since.

But plenty of strong words are used by jockeys, even at televised meetings. It is not surprising with so many runners in the field today there are more incidents and more people are prepared to take risks since the likelihood of them being spotted is less.

I've even known the patrol camera to be wrong. On one occasion at Goodwood I was hauled before the stewards for swerving on my horse in a tight finish. I was second and the stewards held an enquiry, believing I had spoiled the chances of the third horse.

The film of the race was run, it certainly looked on the screen as though my horse had swerved, and after it had been shown the stipendiary steward started to give me a lecture about riding so badly. But I stopped him.

I knew I hadn't swerved on my horse, no matter what the patrol camera might have shown, and towards the end of the film I thought I had spotted the error.

Eph on Premonition, 1953

Winning the Coronation Cup on Aureole at Epsom in 1954

(*Associated Press*)

Aureole winning the Harwick Stake from Janitor at Ascot in 1954

(*P.A.-Reuter*)

'Would you mind running the film through again, sir? I don't think it was my horse that swerved, I think it was the one behind me,' I said.

The steward, Brigadier 'Roscoe' Harvey, looked puzzled, but agreed to run the film again. When it got to the part where my horse appeared to have swerved I asked him to stop the projector and we all looked more closely at the screen.

It had certainly looked to be my horse swerving when the film was run through normally, but the camera had lied. The horse swerving had been the third horse which was in direct line behind me and which had only half shown up on the film. Not until the film was stopped was it clear that there were two horses merging together to look like one—mine.

The stewards therefore allowed the result to stand and exonerated me.

A few of the stewards do not seem to understand a jockey's difficulties, but most of them do. It is owners who create most trouble for jockeys. Today some of them are in it not so much for the sport but for the money and if something goes wrong with what was apparently a good thing they will blame anyone other than the horse or the circumstances of the race.

It has happened to me several times—and to most other jockeys—that although I have been on a horse that could win I have not been able to get it into a position to do so. You can get tucked in a group of runners and quite unable to get out. It's a frustrating thing to have to 'sit and suffer', as we call it, but there isn't much you can do about it unless you want to start barging through with the risk of losing the race on an objection or getting into trouble with the stewards for rough riding.

All you can do is to hope that in time a gap will open

up in front of you or that you will be able to pull out of the pocket and make a good run on the outside. Some jockeys, I think, risk too much by sticking on the rails too long, just hoping that things will break for them. Either that or they don't want to win!

Many owners in racing today do not understand what it is all about. In pre-war days most of the owners were wealthy people in their own right, had usually been brought up to ride and to work with horses and they knew that if a horse was off colour or ran badly in a race it was not necessarily the fault of the trainer or the jockey. They also knew that horses can be extremely temperamental and, just like athletes, footballers, cricketers or anyone else connected with sport, can have their 'off' days.

Some of today's owners have come in through the back door, so to speak, by making fortunes in industry during the war or since and spend enormous sums of money on horses which are not always much good, despite their cost.

When, having spent so much on an animal, they find it does not do well they do not blame the horse—they blame everyone and everything else.

It is not very pleasant for a jockey to come into the unsaddling enclosure on a £5,000 horse which has 'failed again' in a race, to be faced with an angry-looking owner and an obviously embarrassed trainer.

'For God's sake, what went wrong?' is usually the owner's first question.

'I'm sorry, sir, he was just not good enough today,' you say.

The owner turns to the trainer, red-faced: 'I thought you said he was perfectly fit?'

Trainer: 'Oh, he was, he was. But I'm afraid he wasn't quite good enough for today's opposition.'

Ill-tempered owner: 'Well, he ought to be, the price I paid for him. The other horses in the race were all cheap by comparison.'

And he may stalk off to tell his friends that either the trainer or the jockey, or both, are complete fools and he'll get a different trainer for the horse. 'Then we'll get our money back,' he says confidently.

Of course, he doesn't. He's been unlucky. He's bought a pig of a horse who never will be much good, but he doesn't like to accept this. He'll go on running the animal until it drops in the attempt to win, or breaks down.

Candidly there are far too many bad horses in training. Owners will persist with them, despite all advice to the contrary, and not until the poor animals have gone through perhaps three or four trainers and perhaps half a dozen jockeys will it begin to dawn on the owners' minds that the horses never were much good.

Despite the introduction of the race-patrol camera some of the more expensive horses do suffer in racing today. Some races are much rougher than they were before the war, probably because there are so many more runners in each race. Another reason is that there are quite a few more incompetent jockeys riding.

Jockeys seem to be brought up differently now and the whole thing has got very commercialised. When I was an apprentice the older jockeys used to go out of their way to help the younger ones—if the youngsters had any sense at all—and there was a much nicer spirit in the racing game.

As a youngster I received a tremendous amount of good advice about riding from jockeys such as Freddie Fox and Midge Richardson.

When I was with Sneyd, Freddie and Midge used to live not far away at Wantage and they would take it in turns to drive each other to different race meetings. To save money, no doubt. Sneyd fixed up for me to travel with them and it was on these journeys that they used to tell me so much which was to prove helpful in my career.

They both had an enormous fund of knowledge about horses and riding and I feel sure that a lot of the success I had eventually was due to the good advice they had given me.

Now, I'm afraid to say, some of the youngsters seem to think they know it all, don't want to be told anything and, because of this, the older chaps are more reluctant to try to tell them anything in case they get rebuffed.

I have lost my temper many a time since the war with different jockeys for rough riding, jostling and crossing but haven't said, perhaps, as much as I would have liked. A jockey has to be very careful what he says in the dressing room or on the course in case he is called in before the stewards.

Stewards, incidentally, I have always found very fair and many a jockey whose only offence has obviously been over-anxiety to win has been let off with a caution or a nominal fine.

Mind you, certain persistent offenders have been suspended or warned off for diabolical crimes which could be dangerous, and quite rightly so. But they have had to be pretty serious offences for the stewards to be so severe.

Riding in a race is, in some respects, like driving a car in a lot of traffic. Now and again you can hardly help annoying the other chap and breaking the rules. You might suddenly see an opening, dart into it to make progress and in doing so upset the man you have overtaken. Unless it is obviously dangerous driving everyone swears at you for a minute and then forgets all about it.

The same thing applies in racing. You have to take your

advantage when you see it to overtake or cross other horses to get a clear run yourself, and unless it is an extremely reckless move all that happens is that you get sworn at for a minute.

Many things happen which the stewards cannot see, whether it is getting boxed in, baulked, crossed or shoved out of the way, and if it wasn't for the stipendiary stewards who are now posted at various sections of the course I think the conduct of certain jockeys in racing these days would be lamentable. In the olden days, if someone deliberately and repeatedly rode in a rough and unfair way, some of the older jockeys would make it their business to get together and ensure that the same thing happened to the offender. This might have led to trouble for a while, but it usually meant that the persistent chap gave up his tricks when he found the other riders were 'ganging up' on him.

Now, no one dares to 'gang up' and retaliate against a persistently rough rider in case he is caught by the patrol camera or the stipendiary. Consequently, the jockeys who are prepared to take the risk of trouble get away, sometimes, with near murder.

14

A Benefit which Went Wrong

I FEEL very strongly that British jockeys today are riding at a disadvantage compared with their compatriots from the Commonwealth.

Let me say straight away that most of them are very good—they must be good jockeys, otherwise they wouldn't ride so many winners.

But among the jockeys from the home country there is considerable feeling about the way the overseas fellows ride in the finish of a race. A great deal of whispering and talk goes on about it in the dressing room on courses all over the country but no one has actually come out into the open and said it before.

Well, I am going to, as I think the British jockeys have been suffering in silence for long enough.

First let me explain the circumstances.

Australian and other Commonwealth jockeys in this country have a style of riding which is known to us as 'the bobbing style'. It is rather ugly and does not look good horsemanship. The jockeys crouch very low and seem to nod their neads with the horse's movement, keeping a tight hold on the reins and never seeming to work as the English jockeys do when they kick a horse out in the final race for the winning post.

And it is the contrast in this last furlong or so, when

the winning post is approaching, which causes the ill-feeling.

An English jockey absolutely *must* kick his horse out in this final bid for home or at least give every impression of doing so. If he does not, and has perhaps lost a place in the first five or six for not doing so, he will almost certainly be called in before the stewards and accused of not trying. True or not, he could well be 'warned off' for this or at least suspended, so every British jockey will make sure this does not happen and will normally ride as hard as is necessary in the last 200 yards or so.

In contrast to this, the Australian jockeys' style does not usually require them to kick a horse out so obviously. I am not suggesting that they are not trying as hard as their British counterparts. It just *looks* as if they are not. With their hands holding the reins without much slack it does not seem as if they are letting their animals go free to race full out.

The fact that they win a great number of races despite this is clearly a tribute to their supreme riding ability. What I complain about is that the stewards allow them to ride in this ambiguous way, even in a tight finish, when it might *appear* that they are not completely trying.

Why should the stewards make allowances for the Australians doing this when British jockeys would be in trouble if they did the same?

Occasionally you do see the Aussie jockeys really flailing away and letting the reins loose in a tight finish, but not often. Perhaps the answer is that they know, without going all out, just how much to do every time to win, but I can't really believe that. They do get beaten in photo-finishes quite often.

I'm not blaming the jockeys. It is not their fault. It is just their style of riding. But I do blame the stewards for letting them get away with it when not permitting a British jockey to do the same.

The attitude is inconsistent and any inconsistency which would appear to favour one party against another should not be allowed in racing, when so much can be at stake for riders, trainers, owners and punters. However, I suppose it is easy to criticise from a retirement armchair, and I do not intend to say a lot of spiteful things about the profession I have loved and which has given me so much in life. Half the stories about betting jockeys, fixed races and so on are not true anyway.

However, I once rode in a race which I know was fixed and I was the only jockey trying to win. It happened just before the war. I didn't know about this until the race started and, as everything turned out, it was an hilarious affair which went completely wrong.

It was a race in which there were only eight runners, including my horse, a fairly useful animal, but which compared with one or two others should not have stood a chance.

But that was before the jockeys—all except me—decided to have what has been called 'a jockey's race'. They did not let me in on the act because I was supposed to be the winner.

What had happened was that the other seven jockeys had all got together and decided to make a packet on the race with some big betting. They picked the race as being suitable because it was a fairly small field. But it was not too small to prevent getting a good price about the horse they had decided to nominate as the winner: *mine*.

Having just nominated me, they worked it out that they should all appear to be trying but should not, in fact, win.

It didn't take me long to realise from the 'off' that the other riders were having a jockey's benefit.

I had never in my life known such courtesy in a race. For instance, when they thought it was time for me to go into the lead they left an absolutely clear path for me to get through.

They had already ensured that I was in a good position on the rails by pulling out and giving me so much room I could have got a horse-and-cart through. If I started to move out at all on the turn they moved out too to make sure of not crowding me.

It was unbelievable.

When at last I went to the front about two furlongs out I knew everything was being done to let me win. And as I was not in the 'benefit' I thought I had better do everything possible to win in case anything was found out later and I became unwittingly involved.

I rode like mad and for the winning post, but my horse really was not up to it. He started to weaken with about 200 yards to go and, try as I would, I could not make him pick up and go on again.

I heard one of the jockeys shout just behind me, 'Go on, Eph, go on; keep it going.'

But it was no good. My horse was going slower and slower. With only fifty yards to the post another horse ranged alongside me and although I kicked out like mad I could not keep up. The other horse just crept past on the post and I was placed second.

There was such a row as never. It started as we were pulling up.

'What the hell did you want to go and win for?' one jockey hissed at the rider who had won.

'Christ, I couldn't help it. My animal nearly dragged me out of the saddle, it was pulling so hard,' he hissed back.

In the dressing room six sad jockeys looked at the chap who had won as if they could have murdered him.

They had about £2,000 between them on my horse to win. Now it was all lost.

Even the jockey who won had put £300 on me.

I didn't say anything. But I hoped it would teach them a lesson not to try such a thing again. And I must say that was the only time I ever rode in a jockey's benefit, although I believe there have been one or two such races since.

Happily, there are only a few jockeys who would countenance such an idea, and these days, with the patrol camera in operation, it would be exceedingly difficult to succeed.

I did try once refusing to ride a horse at Ascot because I thought the race was 'fixed' and that my animal was among those involved.

It resulted in my having a row with the late Steve Donoghue, for whom I had a third retainer, and I never rode for him afterwards.

Steve had two horses in the race and it never occurred to me that anything was wrong until I received a telephone call the night before. It came from the owner of the horse I was to ride.

'The animal you are riding for me tomorrow is fancied. Don't go tipping it to win,' I was told.

I worried about this call overnight. What did it mean? Who would I tip it to, anyway?

Then I had a look at the other horses entered and noticed the connections were going for the other stable representative. And if this won I realised it could look bad for me, as it did not have the form of my animal at all. It dawned on me that the owner clearly presumed that I would do what I was supposed not to—tip my horse and thus create a market for the other representative. He did not know that I never tipped horses to anyone. When I got to Ascot I saw Steve and told him I didn't want to ride his horse. 'You've got to. I've retained you to ride it,' he said.

I went to see Lord Sefton, senior steward, and told him I didn't feel up to taking the mount.

He looked rather puzzled and also glanced at the clock. 'Well, it's rather late to take you off it now. The declarations have been made.'

I said, 'Well, I'd rather not, if you don't mind, my Lord.'

After holding an enquiry with Donoghue and myself he gave me rather a knowing look. 'Well, Smith,' he said 'we can't really change it now but you don't have to ride for Donoghue in future if you don't want to.'

By then I felt I had made my point. If my horse did not get beaten by the other stable horse any blame likely to be attached to anyone would not fall on to me.

The race? It was another of those which proves that there is no such thing as a racing or betting certainty.

The horse the stable had backed was left at the start. I rode the race of my life, putting everything I could into winning, but it was not good enough. I only finished fourth.

I told Steve I would never ride for him again, but he said nothing to me. An attempt was made by someone purporting to be acting on his behalf to get me to return the £200 as 'third' retainer which I had earlier received from Donoghue, but my solicitor soon put an end to that.

Nothing more was heard of the matter.

One horse which kept getting me into trouble was a very good mount called Set Fair. As a two- and three-year-old he was a top-class sprinter, but as he got older he naturally lost some of his pace.

His trainer, Walter Nightingall, was still keen to run him over five furlongs but he did not win over this distance again. It was suggested two or three times that I had got left at the start on him but I knew this was not correct. The horse just wouldn't go with them and I suggested that he should be run over a longer distance, such as six furlongs, and he went on to win the Diadem Stakes.

At that time I was retained on 'second claim' by Mr. Nightingall, but I did think that one of his principal owners was not too happy with me and I decided not to continue with the retainer after that season.

Candidly, I hated riding for people who I felt were not satisfied with me and rather than ride for them I always gave up any retainer claims.

My last seventeen years with Mr. Joel and Ted Leader could not have been happier, however, as Mr. Joel is the most considerate of owners, has a great understanding of horses and was always most helpful to me.

Mr. Leader is a very even-tempered man and therefore I always found him easy to get along with. He has not always had the best of luck with his horses in training, but he and Mr. Joel have had a long association since Mr. Leader took over the Joel stables at Newmarket from the late Jack Watts.

One of the gamest horses I ever rode was a filly called West Side Story—named after the great musical show had hit London—and she got me into one of the biggest controversies in my racing career.

I had ridden her into second place in the Cheveley Park Stakes and then won the Nell Gwyn Stakes on her at Newmarket. I thought she would have a good chance in the 1,000 Guineas, but without a pacemaker in the race to stretch out all the others she was beaten into third place.

But the controversy really came when she ran in the

1962 Oaks at Epsom. I knew West Side Story could stay, and again, without the pacemaker which I would have liked, I knew I was going to have to make the running for a good part of the race. I went to the front at Tattenham Corner, opened up a big lead, and as my horse just stayed and stayed and had no turn of speed I was praying that nothing would come with a final sprint to catch me.

My prayers were not answered. About a furlong and a half from home a French filly called Monade swooped past and I thought I had had it. But still my filly ran on strongly and gradually, as the winning post got nearer and nearer, the gap between my horse and Monade started to close.

Yves Saint-Martin was doing everything he knew on his filly, while I tried everything in the book to kick West Side Story out a little more. In the last few strides I made up half a length and we crossed the line absolutely together. Another couple of strides past the post and I was in front.

I was convinced I had won. Saint-Martin was equally sure he had won. The judge had announced that there would be a photograph to decide the winner, which usually takes only a couple of minutes to print.

But the seconds and then minutes ticked by and still no result was forthcoming. Bets were continuously being struck on the result, with a dead heat among the most popular choices.

At last, after fourteen minutes, it was announced that Monade had won and that I was second. Changing in the dressing room I could hardly believe my ears. I had been so sure that my horse had fought back to win.

I could not help feeling later after looking at the photo-finish pictures that the result was so close that a 'dead-heat' would have been a fairer result. Monade had just stayed in front, but it was by no more than a whisker—the absolute shortest of short-heads.

Next morning the criticism of my riding came in from several quarters. In the *Daily Telegraph* Marlborough (John Lawrence, the amateur rider) said that I ought to have ridden a waiting race on my horse. Other critics said I should not have been so far in front at Tattenham Corner and that I was caught napping by Saint-Martin.

On the other hand, Saint-Martin was criticised even by M. Jean Lieux, his own trainer, for coming too soon and giving me the chance to get back so much of his lead.

You can't win, can you? It was my view then, and it still is, that the only possible way to ride West Side Story was from the front, unless there was a pacemaker to knock the wind out of any other non-stayers. And I didn't have one.

And how can Saint-Martin be criticised? When he swept past me he would well have thought, with justification, that my horse was nearly beaten and that when in front a furlong from home he could stay there. I was sorry not to have won, for the Oaks is one of the very few important races I have not been able to capture. It has certainly been one of my most unlucky, for this was the fourth time I had finished second in the race and in 1947 and 1959 I had finished third.

15

Ups and Downs

I HAVE had my share of ups and downs in racing, just like everyone else, and some of my downs have been rather painful.

Apart from the fall I had as an apprentice, when I thought my racing days were over, I had three others which were no more pleasant. Strangely enough it was at Windsor, where I had my first winner, that I had my next bad fall, and it put me out of racing for six to eight weeks after I broke three ribs and punctured a lung. On this occasion I was crowded out at the start of a race in which there was a big field and my horse rolled over. I was lucky to get off as lightly as I did.

After this I broke a collar bone and caused Lester Piggott to fall and break a leg when my horse, leading in a mile-and-a-half race, suddenly collapsed with a broken leg. I went down and Lester's mount came on top of us. On this occasion, thanks to Mr. Bill Tucker, the orthopaedic specialist who treats most of the jockeys who suffer fractures in falls, I was back in racing after only ten days.

In a third fall, at Wolverhampton this time, my mount Kishore was one of five horses involved in a pile-up. I sustained a cracked shoulder and fractured wrist. All the other jockeys got away with only bruises, I'm glad to say.

Falls for jockeys are just one of the risks of the trade

and, happily, they do not happen very often on the flat. If they do, it is usually no one's fault and a jockey will do all he can to avoid coming down in front of other horses. One of the worst mishaps in flat racing probably happened when Angers, the French favourite, fell in the Derby along with a crowd of others and caused absolute chaos.

Most jockeys have had bad falls at one time or another and one of the worst affected my brother Doug in the 1964 season, when he suffered a fractured skull. It looked for a while as if he might have been put out of racing for good, but fortunately he made a great recovery and in his last season in 1967 was riding as well as ever.

Doug has always been a very successful jockey. He is a first-class rider, is completely straightforward and he has won the championship five times. He rode first as lightweight jockey for the Aga Khan and Frank Butters after I had loaned him the money to get out of his apprenticeship with the late Major Sneyd. It was the natural thing to do and for many years I was Doug's adviser.

By the time war broke out, Doug had already made a great name for himself as a lightweight jockey and when he was called up and went into the Veterinary Corps he was still able to get away now and again to ride in some races. I once advised Doug not to take a claim as second jockey with Frank Butters. This was during the war years and I was having to take all Doug's bookings and deal with his affairs as a jockey because he was away so much. Mr. Butters was a bit upset that I wouldn't let Doug ride for him as 'second claim', but it worked out right for Doug in the end. After the war he first represented Mr. J. V. Rank, and then rode for the late King George VI and many other famous patrons. His worst period was when he had over a hundred rides without a winner and everybody was saying that he was not riding well. This

(*Fox Photos Ltd.*)

'I refused to shake hands with the Queen!', Ascot, 1958

(*John Slater*)

Eph with his wife and family at their home in Newmarket in 1960

was untrue. A jockey can go through a bad period, just like any sportsman, and when he does, everything seems to go wrong. He will get the worst type of horses to ride and trainers will think he is either out of luck or riding badly and will not give him their best mounts.

One bad thing leads to another and but for the fact that Doug was really a great jockey, and the majority knew it, I don't know what would have happened after he had failed to ride a winner for so long.

Fortunately Doug eventually got back to form and soon was getting as many good rides as ever before, and was winning as many good races.

His greatest ride may well have been in the 1949 Derby, when he was beaten in a photo-finish on a horse called Swallowtail. It was a tremendously thrilling race and although Doug fought furiously on his little horse he was just beaten by Nimbus and Amour Drake in one of the most exciting Derby finishes ever. Doug's run of bad luck had departed before this great race but here again he was unlucky when the photo-finish went against him. It always seems to be the case that if you are out of luck the photo-finish will often not go in your favour.

Coincidence happened to Doug and me during Coronation year, on a day when he was riding in a Coronation Cup race at Haydock Park and I was riding in another Coronation Cup celebration race at Gatwick. We won them both, Doug being successful up North, while I coasted home an easy winner in the South. On another occasion Doug and I swept the board at a race meeting at Kempton. He won four of them and I won the other two, including the winner of the big race of the day. 'The Smith brothers sweep the field' and other complimentary remarks were written and said about us.

Another of our favourite courses has been Yarmouth.

We were always popular there with the holiday crowds and they seemed to follow our fortunes avidly.

I don't know why it just seemed to happen, but Doug and I always pulled off a good number of winners at each meeting there. It was not necessarily the principal meeting of the day, but we always seemed to get booked for rides there and were pleased to take them.

As nearly always happens, success brought more success and we were given more Yarmouth rides with chances of winning. The holiday-makers were pleased no end!

Mind you, Yarmouth was not always a happy course for me. Once I was riding a horse which refused to take the corner, went straight on and deposited me backside first over the fence into a tangle of old barbed wire (I had some difficulty sitting comfortably in the saddle for a few days after that) and on another occasion I was lucky to avoid serious injury when my horse broke a leg and fell in front of several other horses.

I think one of the reasons why Doug and I have always figured in the limelight is because we have always played the thing absolutely straight. Owners have come to trust us and we have been given a very good chance of having a large share in the best rides. The incredible thing is that Doug has not won the Derby.

One of the things Doug and I enjoyed a great deal in our younger days was hunting, and we had a very nice arrangement with the late Mr. Horace Smith, a member of the W. J. Smith Ltd. family who have stables at Holyport which enabled us to get plenty of rides on hunters.

We were then quite well known and whenever Mr. Smith had a hunter or two he wanted to sell he would invite Doug and me to ride them out. It would be a good advertisement for him to have two well-known jockeys on his hunters and we didn't mind being put up in this way because it meant we could have our hunting horses for nothing. Being a farmer's sons, we were allowed during a hunt to stay up fairly close to the huntsmen and, of course, this looked as if Mr. Smith's horses were very good. He didn't have much trouble selling them.

It was also a very good advertisement for his riding school to have us on a couple of his horses. Mind you, we weren't such a good advert as two other of his school's customers during the war—Princess Elizabeth and Princess Margaret.

Doug has always been a great help to me, particularly in sorting out problems due to my faulty hearing. He has travelled with me thousands and thousands of miles, to race meetings in all parts of the country and even as youngsters we stayed together at various hotels or drove each other to the meetings. We have always been very close and very good friends—except during a race, of course. Then we would both try like mad to beat the other. For example, I should have ridden a horse called French Design in the Cesarewitch in 1954. This was a very good animal, but I thought that Harvey Leader had a better horse in training and when he offered me the chance to ride this mount I turned down French Design and put Doug in for the ride. It won for him, my horse finishing nowhere.

Someone has suggested that a book ought to be written about the Racing Smiths. Apart from Doug and myself there is another member of our family equally as good on a horse—our brother Charlie. He's five years older than I and in my opinion he is really one of the best amateur jockeys in the country. He has beaten John Hislop in an amateur flat race at Worcester, defeated Harry Sprague in a hurdle race at Lingfield and he finished in front of

Mr. Gay Kindersley over the fences in a chase at Newbury. He has even won the Town Plate at Newmarket over the flat. Charlie rides at about ten stone and if my father had allowed him to become a professional jockey he would have been among the greatest. (Father at one time was against any of us being jockeys.)

There are not many people in the country who can claim to have won races on the flat, over hurdles *and* over the fences at race meetings all over the country and both Doug and I believe that Charlie is a better jockey than either of us. He certainly has a more impressive all-round record.

16

Oncidium

I WISH the Derby could always have gone as smoothly for me as it did on Blue Peter. But twice in recent years I have been in the spotlight—not for winning, but because of disasters.

The first happened in 1963 when I was to ride a horse called Hullabaloo, trained by Arthur Budgett at Whatcombe, Berks, and owned by Mr. R. N. Richmond-Watson. It was the year Relko, brilliantly ridden by Yves Saint-Martin, slammed the field.

It didn't look as though I was going to have a ride in the big Epsom race at all that year until two days before the Derby, when I was asked by Mr. Budgett if I had a ride fixed. I said 'No' and he asked me to take the ride on Hullabaloo. I didn't know anything about the horse except that it had been second and third in a couple of rather moderate races, but, having nothing else to ride, I thought I might as well take it.

Two hours after accepting I wished I had not, for I received a phone call from Ireland asking me to ride a good three-year-old they had over there called Tarquogan. Having given my word to ride Hullabaloo I could not go back on it, which was a pity because Tarquogan, although he could never have beaten Relko and really didn't quite get a mile and a half, finished a creditable fourth in the Derby, ridden by my friend Willie Snaith.

Anyway Hullabaloo I agreed to ride and a hullabaloo it was. No horse was ever more aptly named. He made me feel and look the biggest fool of all time.

He managed to get through the palaver of the parade in front of the stands and cantered off to the starting gate, but when he got there he created all kinds of trouble. First time in, the start did not come off—if it had done, I think he might have got away well—and we had to line up again. And this time Hullabaloo just refused to get in. He backed, shied away, pranced, danced and almost tried to jump the rails on one occasion. The starter was very patient and gave me several minutes before saying: 'Come along, Smith, you really must get in line.'

Don't think I wasn't trying, but the horse just would not behave. Then Saint-Martin did what I thought was a very sporting thing. He brought Relko back to where Hullabaloo was still darting and diving about and tried to lead my horse in.

I say it was a very sporting gesture of Saint-Martin's and it most certainly was, but I thought he was taking a big risk to do it with Relko, which was not only favourite for the race but a great horse too. With Hullabaloo behaving as he was, Relko might well have been kicked or injured in some way to jeopardise his chances.

One of the things I would like to have done is to have given the horse a damn good hiding with my stick, but before the race Mr. Budgett had told me quite categorically that the horse was not to be touched at any time. Perhaps he had an idea how temperamental it was. So I couldn't get him to behave that way and I couldn't tell the starter's assistant to give him a crack with his hunting crop. After a few minutes it was obvious that I would never get into line.

The other horses were beginning to get restless, waiting

about for my mount and finally, seeing its capers, the starter quite rightly called Saint-Martin back into line and got the race going—fourteen minutes late. I took no part, turned round and, with a struggle, got my horse back to the paddock.

I felt a damn fool having to go back like that on such a big occasion and in front of such an enormous crowd. I was cursing under my breath because obviously it doesn't do one's reputation much good when a thing like that happens, no matter whether one is to blame or not.

I expect Mr. Richmond-Watson was terribly disappointed at the way I failed to get his horse to start and I sympathise with him in his disappointment. Mr. Budgett understood what had happened and I have ridden for him many times since.

Back in the paddock I just handed the horse over to Mr. Budgett's lad, told the trainer what had happened and walked off. I was almost afraid to say much in case I really let fly with a mouthful, but I have no hesitation in saying now that I don't think the horse should ever have been entered for the race. Its price was 100—1 but it might as well have been 1,000—1. It had no chance at all and to my knowledge it never did win a race, either at Epsom or anywhere else.

It is an unfortunate fact—and I'm not saying that these were the circumstances in Hullabaloo's case, because I just don't know—that a lot of owners run horses in the Derby even though they do not have a ghost of a chance of winning.

Why do they do it? I'm not sure, unless it gives them a nice feeling to be able to say: 'I've got a horse running in the Derby.'

In my view it is dangerous to run bad horses in the race with such very good ones and is something which the racing authorities should not allow. Any horse that is entered in the Derby should at least have a reasonable chance of winning and should have shown form in previous high quality races which justify it being accepted as a Derby runner, just as in the Grand National.

Many owners I know would not let a horse run unless it had a reasonable chance, because they would feel if it gave a really terrible display it would do them no credit and would reflect no credit either on the jockey or the trainer.

Another reason is that they might feel a bad horse could easily get in the way of the good ones, cause an accident and generally spoil a race which is supposed to be only for the best three-year-olds in the world.

With so much prize money at stake and considering that their horses might well be worth many thousands of pounds, you would think that owners with the better horses in the race would voice their objections to the bad runners more forcibly than they do. If they did, I think the qualifications I have mentioned would be introduced.

The other Derby sensation in which I figured was of far more consequence for me and it resulted in my being severely criticised in some sections of the racing Press. If ever criticism was unjustified this was, but it did not help my feelings at the time to know this, particularly as I was nursing the disappointment of the result for many days after the race had been run.

The horse was called Oncidium and many thousands of pounds had been put on him to win by punters all over the country. All were disappointed. The punters had, in fact, backed the horse down to second favourite at 9—2, and up to the time of the race they had every reason to be confident.

It may not be any comfort to them now, but I'll explain

as well as I can why it was that Oncidium did not win the Derby of 1964, as so many expected.

Oncidium was a pig of a horse. He had a kink. There are no other words I can find to describe him and I hope that his owner, Lord Howard de Walden, and his original trainer, Mr. Jack Waugh, at Newmarket, will forgive me for calling him that if they still have any affection for him.

But that is how I found him and, I say with some regret, how he appeared to turn out for another famous jockey, the Australian Scobie Breasley.

If ever a horse led you up the garden path then Oncidium did. If I had been a betting jockey—which, thank God, I am not and never have been (that is why I've got some money in the bank)—then I think I would have put my shirt on Oncidium to win the Derby despite the fact that he had some great horses to compete with, such as Santa Claus and Indiana.

I was as confident about winning the Derby on Oncidium as I had been on Blue Peter, provided I had a decent run. In the event, he gave me the most disappointing ride I have ever had.

Oncidium was first ridden by me at Sandown as a three-year-old. He had previously been ridden by that very fine jockey Stan Smith who, incidentally, is no relation, but Stan had a nasty fall at Epsom, injured his shoulder, and was out for quite some time.

Therefore, when I rode him in the Royal Stakes over a mile and a quarter at Sandown I had never ridden him before and was delighted when he won quite easily like a good horse.

Harry Carr had ridden him as a two-year-old and the horse had done nothing outstanding, so this form was rather a surprise to his connections. In fact, as a two-year-old he had swerved and swung about all over the place.

Then Oncidium won the Lingfield Derby Trial and it was a shattering win.

During the race about a mile from home he suddenly raised his head and faltered and I thought he must have got some dirt in his face from the horses running in front. So I pulled him to the outside and he picked up the bit and really streaked home, to win by six lengths in a canter.

Indiana was fifth, at least ten lengths behind.

After the Sandown race Jack Waugh had asked me if I would like to ride him in the Derby and I was so impressed with his performance that I said I would love to. Now, after the Lingfield victory, he seemed to have a wonderful chance of pulling off the 'big un'.

I had the misfortune to be drawn No. 1 in the Derby, which is considered a bad draw, but I was not too worried about it because I felt that Oncidium had plenty of stamina and speed to overcome that little handicap. I was satisfied I would be able to take up a nice position whenever I wanted to.

After half a mile I knew that I wasn't going to win. Oncidium's behaviour was bewildering. He seemed a completely different horse to the one I had ridden on the two previous occasions.

He was dropping his bit all the time and not taking any interest in the race at all. I thought he must have been getting dirt in his face again and pulled out from the rails, but it didn't make the slightest bit of difference.

He constantly hung his head to the right, away from the rails, and I knew he was going very badly. In front of me, setting the pace, was a horse ridden by Geoff Lewis, called Hotroy. It was trained by Walter Nightingall at Epsom and was going much better than mine, whereas in the

Lingfield Trial it had run so badly it could not even make the running. I ought to have had Oncidium on a tight rein by now, with him pulling for his head, but he just went along in a listless fashion and nothing I did could make him go properly.

Despite all this, before we reached Tattenham Corner we were lying third and at the famous corner we were in front. I knew we stood no chance at all unless Oncidium picked up the bit there and then—we were only in this position because none of the other horses were really trying at that stage—but he did not, and, sure enough, after a furlong in the straight, we had been passed by several horses, including Indiana. It was infuriating. A moment before I had had a perfectly clear run with nothing at all in front of me. Yet here I was on a horse which if he tried had fantastic speed and even at that late stage might have been able to win. But he would not budge. I tried everything I knew to make him run on, but he just swished his head from side to side and plodded on.

In the last furlong Santa Claus swept by with an incredible burst of speed to snatch the race from Indiana.

Scobie Breasley was criticised for his riding by some people. It was said that he had left his run very late and should never have been nearly last coming down the hill into Tattenham Corner. Other critics said that he had ridden a perfectly judged race, that he knew the horse's capabilities and was therefore entitled to win as he liked. Well, he did win and that was as good an answer to the moaners as anything I know.

On the other hand, if Oncidium had run as well as at Lingfield and taken some interest in the race I think Scobie might have had reason to regret his position at Tattenham Corner. He certainly covered the last two furlongs with a blistering run on the outside, but if Oncidium had been going hell for leather at the same time, with such an advantage at Tattenham Corner I don't think he would have been caught.

There were no recriminations for me from either Mr. Waugh or Lord Howard de Walden, disappointed though they were. Mr. Waugh just said: 'Don't worry, Eph. I saw what happened in the straight when he was shaking his head.'

But in the Press next day several of the racing correspondents said I had ridden a bad race on the course. Some alleged that I had come to the front too soon, while others thought I had not done as well as I should trying to get him going.

I had to suffer in silence.

I rode Oncidium in the St. Leger, but again I could not get much life out of him, although he did finish fifth. He certainly had a kink. We tried him twice with blinkers on the gallops, but he wouldn't go with them on either. He was a complete enigma.

Before the Leger, Mr. Waugh had suggested to Lord Howard de Walden that perhaps the horse was fed up with its surroundings at Newmarket and it might be a good idea to change trainers. The horse was then sent to George Todd at his stables at Manton, Wilts.

Oncidium ran in another race that season in the Jockey Club when, in poor company, he managed to win. This time Scobie Breasley rode him.

However, next season he was a changed horse again for a while. He came out first time to win the Coronation Cup during Derby week at Epsom in such style that everyone started to say how Mr. Todd had worked wonders with him, how it took a good jockey to ride him and what a wonderful horse he was. Well, on that showing he was, and it began to look rather bad for Jack Waugh and myself.

Oncidium was then entered in one of the richest races of the year, the Gold Cup over two and a half miles at Ascot.

On his Epsom form he looked 'a good thing' and started at evens favourite. But he got up to his old tricks again. He hung his head to the left, refused to take up the bit and finished fourth, well behind Fighting Charlie, the winner, ridden by Lester Piggott and the second, a French horse called Waldmeister. And this time poor old Scobie got into trouble with the critics who said he stayed too far back in the early stages and gave Oncidium too much to do at the finish.

I could sympathise with Scobie. I knew how frustrated he must have been when the horse refused to take any interest in the racing.

Oncidium only won once again that season, in a two-horse race at Goodwood when he made all the running. He was beaten into third place at Ascot by Super Sam and Soderini in the John Collier Stakes—he had easily beaten Soderini at level weights in the Coronation Cup—and finished third in the King George VI and Queen Elizabeth Stakes, again at Ascot, when Lester Piggott won on Meadow Court.

After the Derby I wondered for a long time whether he might have been doped, as he had run so badly, but I now know that this was not the case.

He was just infuriatingly difficult. If he had shown a consistent interest in racing he would have been among the great. As it was, the only thing you could do was try to forget him and hope never to get another like him.

17

Other Jockeys

JOCKEYS have always been keen on a good party. Whether it be the plush celebration parties they have each year for the champion jockey at the Savoy, or whether it is just a few drinks in the local pub, they just love to get together and enjoy a few drinks and some 'shop' talk. Before the war the champion jockey always threw and paid for a big party, but now all the jockeys contribute although those who ride more than 100 winners in a season pay a larger share of the cost.

In 1966 I was honoured, with the late Bill Elliott, to be given a farewell party at the Savoy and had as my guests Lord Rosebery and Mr. H. J. Joel. I was presented by the jockeys with a silver salver and enjoyed a splendid evening with my old colleagues.

They are generally a good-hearted crowd and, like many other sportsmen, take every available opportunity to have a bit of fun. One of the biggest jokers was Tommy Weston and I remember how he scared the life out of Cliff Richards, brother of Sir Gordon, during a race at Warwick. He pinched his bottom!

I laughed so much I nearly fell off.

There was a huge field in the race, over a mile and a quarter, and the horses were all packed tightly together going down the hill.

Weston was in the middle of a pretty tight bunch, with

Cliff just in front of him, and wanted badly to get through. But he couldn't make it.

So he reached out and gave Cliff a determined tweak. Poor Cliff, he thought for a minute that a horse was trying to savage him. He gave his animal a kick to streak away out of range, and Tommy thus got the opening he wanted.

Of course, it's not really the 'done thing' in racing to try something like that, but I must admit I used the trick myself once on Willie Snaith under similar circumstances. I don't think it would be possible to get away with it now, as the race-patrol camera would probably pick out the offender, with serious consequences.

Weston was one of the great characters of racing. Somehow, in a tight finish, he would always lose his cap (in the days before jockeys wore crash helmets). Whether he did it on purpose or not I don't know, but it was a most effective method of indicating he was trying like mad to win and usually earned a cheer from the crowd, whatever the result.

In the dressing room there is usually quite a lot of leg-pulling, and Lester Piggott, who takes racing very seriously, is often the butt of some of the humorists, who look at the game with a little less intensity. He usually takes the jokes with a sniff of disdain or a grunt, quite content to wait until a race gets under way to get his own back.

As youngsters we were always getting up to something together and I remember when we were up North to ride at Liverpool a group of us decided to try to save some money by cooking our meals over the fire in our bedroom at the Stork Hotel. There were four of us sharing the room, Frankie Hudson, Bill and Fred Rickaby and myself, and Fred decided it would be a good idea if we cooked a massive omelette. We put a match to the fire, which had probably not been lit for years, broke about a dozen eggs to make the omelette and placed it on the fire. For a minute our attention was distracted, and the next thing we knew a pile of soot had come down the chimney and landed slap-bang in the middle of the frying-pan. Bits of omelette flew all over the marble washstand and the fireplace, and it looked as though we had been having a battle with the stuff. It put an end to our aspirations as chefs, for we had to spend half the night clearing up the mess, fearful of the reaction from the hotel manager if he walked in and saw the room looking as though someone had been having an omelette Aunt Sally game in it.

But jockeys are always having trouble over eating, often because of weight problems but also because of the sad conditions under which they have to work. Even these days some of the amenities are quite deplorable and the catering is so bad at some courses you cannot even get a decent cup of tea. However, things are gradually improving on a number of courses.

For instance, Ascot now has very nice changing rooms for the jockeys, and at Epsom and Sandown the amenities are also good. It is at the lesser race courses that a great deal needs to be done where the conditions are lamentable. The jockeys sometimes have to change in a small hut, there are inadequate toilet and washing facilities, and the catering is also under par. Jockeys have to rush from course to course these days, particularly when there are evening as well as day meetings, and consequently they have to grab meals wherever and whenever they can. If canteen arrangements on the race courses are bad the jockeys often finish up with indigestion. It really is not good enough.

One must not be too critical, however, for there have been dramatic improvements in racing itself in latter years, and the introduction of the patrol camera, stipendiary stewards along the course at suitable positions, and various efforts to improve the courses themselves—they are being given plenty of peat to keep them soft and in good condition—have all gone to improve the image of racing in the 1960s.

The general standard of riding is gradually improving, and there are some very useful young jockeys, like Paul Cook, coming to the fore. But ten jockeys stand out in my mind as having been exceptional during my career. I'll list them in alphabetical order.

Beary, Michael. The little Irishman was the most polished horseman I have seen. He had a tremendous 'feel' for an animal and, given time to show his patience with a horse, could turn a bad 'un into a potential winner.

Breasley, A. 'Scobie'. I've already said that I do not much like the style of riding of the Australian jockeys these days, but whether I like it or not, it seems to be successful, as Scobie has proved. He is very good at coming through on the rails to snatch a dramatic win.

Carslake, Brownie. This Australian jockey was absolutely first class in a finish. If he was in the running he rarely got beaten and his timing and judgment in a race were quite unmatched by anyone I have seen before or since. It was a tragedy when he died quite young.

Lindley, Jimmy. He has been worried with over-weight troubles, which cut him down to 347 mounts in 1965. But his judgment is not impaired by this and in the big races he has proved highly successful, as demonstrated when he won the St. Leger on Indiana in 1964 and the 2,000 Guineas in 1966.

Mercer, Joe. He climbed to second place in the jockeys'

table in 1965 and may well take over from Lester as champion one day. His great asset: He can ride in any race, over any distance, with equal coolness.

Piggott, Lester. Only the weight problem, which he has every year and which prevents him riding as many horses as he should, stops his tally of winners going to astronomical heights. He has tremendous confidence and strength and his all consuming ambition is to ride winners, more winners, and even more winners, and I think it is marvellous that he keeps his weight down to the 8 st. 3 lb. mark to ride as many horses as possible. He was champion jockey in 1965 with 160 winners and it is very significant that out of his 580 mounts in the season he was placed 311 times.

Richards, Gordon, was a law unto himself and no one could copy his style. I tried to myself once, but I couldn't do it. In his early days he used to swerve about a bit, but he got on top of that and he could get a horse first past the post with tremendous power. His determination and ambition to win somehow carried him on when others might have thought the race was lost. He could judge the pace of a race well and his tally of over 4,000 winners has never been equalled in Britain.

Smirke, Charlie. What can you say about this man who has won the Derby more times than any other jockey? Only one thing—he was a great jockey because he had all the confidence and cheek in the world. Charlie would take the most outrageous chances with a horse which to most riders could have meant only certain defeat. The difference with Charlie was that, having taken these chances, he still won.

Smith, Doug. The great asset about my brother's riding is that he is equally as good in a race of any distance, long, medium or short. He is upright, conscientious and hard-working and has been rewarded with the championship five times.

Wragg, Harry. He taught me so much about judging pace and distance and, as the 'Headwaiter', knew precisely when to get his animal going to come and win from behind.

Somewhere in this bunch, I'm told, the name of Eph Smith ought to figure. At least, the Press reports have said a few times that I was one of the 'top ten' jockeys and it is not for me to judge. Perhaps my name should figure along with Michael Beary's, for like him I've always tried to be as much a horseman as a professional racing jockey.

Two other jockeys I would like to mention are Steve Donoghue and Charlie Elliott. Steve belonged to the 'old school' of riding and was at his peak just before I came on the scene. He was a quiet, easy rider, with wonderful hands and was especially good on two-year-olds. Charlie was a very good all-round jockey, with a fine style, and had a wonderful temperament for the big occasion.

A non-English jockey I have admired, and who gave the perfect example of courageous riding in the Derby of 1965, is Pat Glennon. He won so easily on Sea Bird, despite moving out quite early on in the straight, and just swept past the opposition. Of course, he had a really good horse to do it with, but many jockeys I know would have been afraid to take the chance so soon. He emphasised the whole point to racing: if you know your horse is good enough to win then why hesitate or hold back?

It sometimes takes courage to ride in this way, but in racing, as in everything else, boldness favours the brave. I hope it always will.

18

After Thirty-seven Years . . .

MY decision to retire from racing may have surprised many followers, trainers and owners. I had said at the end of the 1965 season that, although I was going to part from Mr. Joel and his trainer Ted Leader, I was going to be a freelance jockey and would look around in every direction for as many rides as I could get. I thought that after seventeen years it was only fair to give Mr. Joel the chance to get a younger jockey.

This may have seemed a strange decision to those who knew that in thirty-seven years of racing I had never had more than two first retainers (Jack Jarvis and Mr. Joel), but I also thought I might get more winning rides as a freelance.

Mr. Joel was not always the most fortunate owner, but he was the most understanding and considerate. He would spend a great deal of money on horses with the necessary Classic breeding to win a number of really good races, but they did not come up to scratch as often as they ought to have done on average.

The son of a famous owner and gambler, the late Mr. Jack Joel, who won the 1911 Derby with Sunstar, Mr. H. J. Joel is the nephew of Mr. Solly Joel, who had an incredible number of good winners in his time.

I was always sorry that Mr. H. J. Joel did not have

better luck with his animals, because he is such a tremendous lover of the turf and an enthusiastic owner, and it was therefore a wonderful thrill for me when we did have great success with one of his horses called Predominate.

Anyone who follows racing will remember this fine animal. It achieved something which, I believe, has never been equalled and is hardly likely to be: winning the Goodwood Stakes three years in succession.

This is always a tough race and from winning in 1958 with a fairly light weight, it went on to win next year carrying nearly a stone more. And he won yet again in 1960 carrying top weight.

In 1961 he proved what a game horse he was by winning the Goodwood Cup, despite the fact that he broke down in the race.

I remember that this happened with about a mile to go and I thought my chances were absolutely finished. However, despite suffering a leg injury, he battled on to win by a short head.

This was his last race and he had to be retired. But for the injury I think he might well have gone on to win the Goodwood Cup again the following year.

It was certainly my intention right up the close of the season of 1965 to carry on riding, but then I was taken ill at the end of the year. The doctors said I was suffering from nervous exhaustion and I reluctantly decided that the only fair thing for owners, trainers and myself was to give up. I thought it was better to go out near the top than slip down to the bottom. Over the last few years, travelling and the wear and tear of racing itself were among the factors contributing towards my failing health.

Once upon a time, a jockey knew well in advance what

his rides were going to be for the various meetings. But nowadays the trainers are not able, because of the advent of declarations, to give the several days' notice that jockeys once received regarding the horses they are to ride.

Therefore, on Sundays you have trainers ringing up jockeys, jockeys ringing up owners, and owners ringing back to trainers and jockeys to try to find out what horses each wants the other to ride and what mounts they are available to ride.

A trainer may suddenly decide he wants his retained jockey to ride in a particular race and the jockey may then have to ring up another trainer or owner to ask to be released from another horse in the same race. It is all rather confusing.

But for my wife Doreen I don't know where I should have been. Although I have an amplifier on our telephone, I have not always been able to understand what people have said to me on the phone.

Consequently in latter years, when there have been telephone calls from people trying to book me for rides, it has been Doreen who has taken the brunt of all the work. But for her I should probably have spent half the time riding the wrong horse at the wrong meetings in the wrong races!

For me, it has become too business-like. To be a sportsman or a good jockey is insufficient. Jockeys are working seven days a week to ride in races or drive from one course to another and ride gallops. They have to live in hotels or fly, which is really expensive, from the South to the North of England, or from east to west. On the remaining day they always seem to be answering the telephone.

So after I had recovered in hospital, and the doctors

told me to quit, I decided that they were probably giving very good advice.

But I am satisfied. After thirty-seven years I've retired quite comfortably off with a reputation for being straight and with hundreds of extremely happy and worthwhile memories.

You cannot ask for much more than that in any career, can you?

EPH SMITH—RIDING RECORD

	Wins	*Rides*	*Big Race Successes*
1930	7	79	
1931	10	188	
1932	34	395	Great Metropolitan H'cap—ROI DE PARIS
			Hwfa Williams Mem. H'cap—BOLDERO
1933	52	561	King Edward VII Stakes—SANS PEINE
			Windsor Castle Stakes—CAMPANULA
			Goodwood Cup—SANS PEINE
			West of Scotland Trial H'cap—APPLE PEEL
1934	36	502	Free Handicap (3 y.o.)—PHALERON BAY
			Salford Borough Handicap—SUDAN
			Queen Anne Stakes—SPEND A PENNY
			Northumberland Plate—WHITEPLAINS
			Bibury Cup—NORMAN HERALD
			West of Scotland Trial H'cap—PIP EMMA
			Ayrshire Handicap—NORMAN HERALD
			Caledonian Hunt Cup—PIP EMMA
			Manchester November H'cap—PIP EMMA
1935	76	753	Brocklesby Stakes—TETRAZONE
			Lincolnshire Handicap—FLAMENCO
			Wokingham Stakes—THEIO
			July Stakes—DAYTONA
			Welsh Derby—BIDEFORD BAY
			Gordon Stakes—BIDEFORD BAY
			Cesarewitch—NEAR RELATION
			Free Handicap (3 y.o.)—TEWKESBURY
1936	80	778	Great Metropolitan H'cap—JACK TAR
			Esher Cup—SILVER CREST
			Oaks Trial Stakes—MISS WINDSOR
			Britannia Stakes—EDGEHILL
			Windsor Castle Stakes—THE HOUR

	Wins	*Rides*	*Big Race Successes*
			Northumberland Plate—COUP DE ROI
			Stewards Cup—SOLERINA
			Nottingham Stewards H'cap—SOLERINA
			Newbury Autumn Cup—COUP DE ROI
1937	78	832	Column Produce Stakes—GAINSBOROUGH LASS
			March Stakes—BONSPIEL
			Ascot Gold Vase—FEARLESS FOX
			Coronation Stakes—GAINSBOROUGH LASS
			Gosforth Park Cup—HARMACHIS
			Goodwood Cup—FEARLESS FOX
			Edinburgh Gold Cup—EDGEHILL
			Dewhurst Stakes—MANORITE
			Liverpool St. Leger—DHARAMPUR
1938	114	836	Brocklesby Stakes—CANTICLE
			Lincolnshire Handicap—PHAKOS
			Craven Stakes—CHALLENGE
			Blue Riband Trial Stakes—CHATSWORTH
			Victoria Cup—PHAKOS
			Payne Stakes—FLYON
			Ascot Stakes—FRAWN
			Churchill Stakes—INSCRIBE
			Goodwood Stakes—SNAKE LIGHTNING
			Chesterfield Cup—PYLON II
			Scottish Derby—FAERIE QUEEN
			Ayr Gold Cup—OLD RELIANCE
			Caledonian Hunt Cup—APHRODOSIA
			Jockey Club Stakes—CHALLENGE
			Newmarket St. Leger—FLYON
			Newmarket Oaks—FAERIE QUEEN
			Challenge Stakes—OLD RELIANCE
			Hwfa Williams Mem. H'cap—INSCRIBE
			Liverpool St. Leger—FLYON
1939	70	641	Blue Riband Trial Stakes—BLUE PETER

	Wins	Rides	Big Race Successes
			2,000 Guineas—BLUE PETER
			DERBY—BLUE PETER
			White Rose Stakes—HUNTER'S MOON IV
			Newbury Summer Cup—TOUT CHANGE
			Ascot Stakes—FRAWN
			St. James's Palace Stakes—ADMIRAL'S WALK
			Bessborough Stakes—ALISTAIR
			Ascot Gold Cup—FLYON
			Cork and Orrery Stakes—OLD RELIANCE
			Eclipse Stakes—BLUE PETER
			Manchester November H'cap—TUTOR
1940	37	328	Subs Champion Stakes—HIPPIUS
1941	61	408	White Rose Stakes (Newbury)—HIPPIUS
			Nottingham Stewards H'cap—ZAITOR
			Edinburgh Gold Cup—CONGRATULATIONS
			Subs Champion Stakes—HIPPIUS
1942	52	300	Subs Nunthorpe Stakes—LINKLATER
			Subs Middle Park Stakes—RIBBON
			Jockey Club Cup—AFTERTHOUGHT
1943	33	268	Subs Coronation Cup—HYPERIDES
			Subs Nunthorpe Stakes—LINKLATER
1944	32	280	Column Produce Stakes—OCEAN SWELL
			Free Handicap (3 y.o.)—ROADHOUSE
			Jockey Club Cup—OCEAN SWELL
1945	66	371	Newmarket Stakes—MIDAS
			Ascot Gold Cup—OCEAN SWELL
			July Cup—HONEYWAY
			Princess of Wales Stakes—STIRLING CASTLE
			Prince of Wales Stakes—EASTERN IMP
			Challenge Stakes—ROYAL CHARGER

	Wins	*Rides*	*Big Race Successes*
1946	112	657	Victoria Cup—HONEYWAY
			Yorkshire Cup—STIRLING CASTLE
			Oaks Trial Stakes—IONA
			Queen Anne Stakes—ROYAL CHARGER
			Ascot Stakes—REYNARD VOLANT
			Royal Hunt Cup—FRIAR'S FANCY
			Cork and Orrery Stakes—HONEYWAY
			Rous Memorial Stakes—HOBO
			July Stakes—MISS STRIPES
			Bibury Cup—BRISTOL FASHION
			Nassau Stakes—WAYWARD BELLE
			City and Suburban H'cap—HOBO
			Brighton Cup—HEAD WORKER
			Ayr Gold Cup—ROYAL CHARGER
			Goodwood Stakes—REYNARD VOLANT
			Brown Jack Stakes—ACCELERATION
			Champion Stakes—HONEYWAY
			Midland Cesarewitch—LADY CRUSADER
1947	114	753	Free Handicap (4 y.o.)—HIGHLAND LADDIE
			Ascot Stakes—REYNARD VOLANT
			Duke of Cambridge H'cap—PAPER WEIGHT
			Bibury Cup—BRIDLE PATH
			Falmouth Stakes—MERMAID
			Liverpool Summer Cup—SWISS FLOWER
			Brighton Cup—HEAD WORKER
			Lanark Silver Bell—PARHELION
1948	112	778	City and Suburban H'cap—FAST SOAP
			Esher Cup—ASMAN TARA
			March Stakes—SICAVO
			Great Northern Stakes—BENNY LYNCH
			July Cup—PALM VISTA
			Stewards Cup—DRAMATIC
			Liverpool Summer Cup—FIGHTER COMMAND

	Wins	*Rides*	*Big Race Successes*
			West of Scotland Trial H'cap—CAPPIELLUCCA
			Champion Stakes—SOLAR SLIPPER
			Midland Cambridgeshire—WISLEY
1949	74	582	Lincolnshire Handicap—FAIR JUDGEMENT
			Esher Cup—SPY LEGEND
			Woodcote Stakes—FULL DRESS
			Rose of York Sweepstakes—STEROPE
			Park Hill Stakes—SEA IDOL
			Cesarewitch—STRATHSPEY
1950	88	750	Rosebery Stakes—ROMAN WAY
			1,000 Guineas Trial Stakes—SANLINEA
			Classic Trial Stakes (Thirsk)—MASKED LIGHT
			Lancashire Oaks—DUTCH CLOVER
			Manchester Cup—LAKE PLACID
			King George V H'cap Stakes—COASTAL WAVE
			King's Stand Stakes—TANGLE
			Yorkshire Oaks—ABOVE BOARD
			Cesarewitch—ABOVE BOARD
1951	58	495	Ascot Gold Vase—FAUX PAS
			Falmouth Stakes—RED SHOES
			Criterion Stakes—QUEEN OF LIGHT
1952	81	620	1,000 Guineas Trial—LADY SOPHIA
			King George V H'cap Stakes—GIULIANO
			July Cup—SET FAIR
			Falmouth Stakes—QUEEN OF LIGHT
			Great Yorkshire H'cap—GIULIANO
			Gordon Carter H'cap—FRENCH DESIGN
			Diadem Stakes—SET FAIR
			Liverpool Autumn Cup—KING CARDINAL
1953	84	675	Great Northern Stakes—PREMONITION

	Wins	Rides	Big Race Successes
			Coronation Festival Stakes (Birmingham)—SET FAIR
			Chesham Stakes—HIGH TREASON
			Windsor Castle Stakes—KING'S EVIDENCE
			Prince of Wales Stakes—KING'S EVIDENCE
			Great Yorkshire Stakes—WYANDANK
			ST. LEGER—PREMONITION
			Cumberland Lodge Stakes—AUREOLE
			Hwfa Williams Mem. H'cap—FRENCH DESIGN
1954	76	636	Coronation Cup—AUREOLE
			Ascot Gold Vase—PRESCRIPTION
			Hardwicke Stakes—AUREOLE
			Princess of Wales Stakes—WOODCUT
			King George VI & Queen Elizabeth Stakes—AUREOLE
			Gordon Stakes—BRILLIANT GREEN
			Knight's Royal Stakes—UMBERTO
			Jockey Club Stakes—BRILLIANT GREEN
			Solario Stakes—NORTH CONE
			Criterion Stakes—STATE TRUMPETER
			Midland Cesarewitch—WINDLESS
1955	82	579	Brocklesby Stakes—VERMEIL
			Ormonde Stakes—NORTH CONE
			Britannia Stakes—CRONUS
			Oxfordshire Stakes—TRUE CAVALIER
			Prince of Wales Stakes (York)—STAR OF INDIA
			Rose of York Sweepstakes—DARIUS
			Prince Edward H'cap—THE BLACK HORSE
			Midland Cambridgeshire—OPERA SCORE
1956	74	537	Wood Ditton Stakes—FULL MEASURE

	Wins	*Rides*	*Big Race Successes*
			City of Birmingham Cup—TRENT BRIDGE
			Lancashire Oaks—HUSTLE
			Princess of Wales Stakes—CASH AND COURAGE
			Stewards Cup—MATADOR
			Prince of Wales Stakes (York)—PICTURE LIGHT
			Stanley Ford Stakes—MATADOR
			Rufford Abbey H'cap—CASSIS
			Cambridgeshire—LOPPYLUGS
1957	70	485	Dee Stakes—PALOR
			Lonsdale Produce (Epsom)—MAJOR PORTION
			Lancashire Oaks—LOBELIA
			Coventry Stakes—AMERIGO
			Cork and Orrery Stakes—MATADOR
			Chesham Stakes—MAJOR PORTION
			National Breeders Produce Stakes PROMULGATION
			Richmond Stakes—PROMULGATION
			Middle Park Stakes—MAJOR PORTION
1958	71	496	Free Handicap (3 y.o.)—FAULTLESS SPEECH
			Rosebery Memorial H'cap—LUCKY WHITE HEATHER
			St. James's Palace Stakes—MAJOR PORTION
			Rous Memorial Stakes—SNOW CAT
			Sussex Stakes—MAJOR PORTION
			Goodwood Stakes—PREDOMINATE
			Princess Mary Nursery—YUCATAN
			Queen Elizabeth II Stakes—MAJOR PORTION
			Midland Cambridgeshire—SMALL SLAM
1959	79	547	Ascot Stakes—RUGOSA
			Britannia Stakes—MACQUARIO

	Wins	*Rides*	*Big Race Successes*
			Rous Memorial Stakes—PINICOLA
			Falmouth Stakes—CRYSTAL PALACE
			Cherry Hinton Stakes—PANGA
			Molecomb Stakes—QUEENSBERRY
			Goodwood Stakes—PREDOMINATE
			Nassau Stakes—CRYSTAL PALACE
			Oxfordshire Stakes—KALYDON
			Lowther Stakes—QUEENSBERRY
			Park Hill Stakes—COLLYRIA
			Rufford Abbey H'cap—PREDOMINATE
			Cheveley Park Stakes—QUEENSBERRY
			Dewhurst Stakes—ANCIENT LIGHTS
1960	62	497	Brocklesby Stakes—INDIAN LAD
			1,000 Guineas Trial, Kempton—QUEENSBERRY
			Royal Standard Stakes—OFF KEY
			Jersey Stakes—RED GAUNTLET
			Queen Alexandra Stakes—PREDOMINATE
			Goodwood Stakes—PREDOMINATE
			Fifinella Stakes (Epsom)—RECKLESS
			Horris Hill Stakes—GALLANT KNIGHT
1961	50	417	Union Jack Stakes—SEAM
			Newbury Spring Cup—ZANZIBAR
			Dante Stakes—GALLANT KNIGHT
			Goodwood Cup—PREDOMINATE
			Oxfordshire Stakes—SAGACITY
			Rose of York H'cap—ZANZIBAR
			Solario Stakes—HIDDEN MEANING
			Ayr Gold Cup—KLONDYKE BILL
			Cesarewitch—AVONS PRIDE
1962	61	460	Nell Gwyn Stakes (Newmarket)—WEST SIDE STORY
			Queen's Prize—MINUTE GUN
			1,000 Guineas Trial, Kempton—HIDDEN MEANING
			Great Metropolitan H'cap—NARRATUS
			Cheshire Oaks—TROPIC STAR

	Wins	*Rides*	*Big Race Successes*
			St. James's Palace Stakes—COURT SENTENCE
			Windsor Castle Stakes—SUMMER DAY
			Princess of Wales Stakes—SILVER CLOUD
			Yorkshire Oaks—WEST SIDE STORY
			Gt. Yorkshire H'cap—ILLUMINOUS
			Prince of Wales Nursery—SALTARELLO
			Royal Lodge Stakes—STAR MOSS
			Cheveley Park Stakes—MY GOODNESS ME
			Middle Park Stakes—CROCKET
1963	44	374	John Porter Stakes—PETER JONES
			Rous Memorial Stakes—FAIR ASTRONOMER
			Ripon St. Leger Trial—STAR MOSS
			Yorkshire Oaks—OUTCROP
			Galtres Stakes—TURF
			Park Hill Stakes—OUTCROP
			Brighton Autumn Cup—OSIER
1964	27	311	Midlands Spring H'cap—MANDAMUS
			Royal Stakes (Sandown)—ONCIDIUM
			Lingfield Derby Trial—ONCIDIUM
			Great Yorkshire H'cap (Doncaster) PHILEMON
1965	25	222	Golden Hind Stakes (Ascot) ARDENT DANCER
			Pretty Polly Stakes (Newmarket)—MIBA
			Matador H'cap—PASSPORT
			Kirk & Kirk Stakes—MARANDIS
			Duke of Edinburgh Stakes—PERSIAN EMPIRE
	2313	18401	Big Race Successes—269